Developing Successful
Business Strategies

Developing Successful Business Strategies

Gaining the Competitive Advantage

Rob Reider

BEP BUSINESS EXPERT PRESS

First published in 2015 by
Business Expert Press, LLC
222 East 46th Street, New York, NY 10017
www.businessexpertpress.com

ISBN-13: 978-1-63157-079-7 (paperback)
ISBN-13: 978-1-63157-080-3 (e-book)

Business Expert Press Strategic Management Collection

Collection ISSN: 2150-9611 (print)
Collection ISSN: 2150-9646 (electronic)

Cover and interior design by Exeter Premedia Services Private Ltd., Chennai, India

First edition: 2015

10 9 8 7 6 5 4 3 2 1

Printed in the United States of America.

Abstract

This book presents effective planning of business strategies and related budgeting concepts, and those activities necessary for the successful growth of the organization. The planning process is shown to be an integral function of developing management strategies for future growth and the gaining of competitive advantage in these fast moving times. Budgeting is presented as a logical outgrowth and an essential part of the planning process rather than an independent internal activity. The book emphasizes the principal factors that should be considered in planning and budgeting for the company, what management and operations personnel must know to better understand effective planning for the business, and what can be done to enhance the overall strategic and financial planning for the organization.

The intent of the book is to introduce and explain the relationship between effective planning methods (long-term and short-term) and the budgeting and control processes. The program concentrates on practical approaches to organizational planning and integration with budgeting as well as enhancing familiarity with related concepts and methodology. The book is designed for those who desire to increase their knowledge and practical use of planning and budgeting techniques as a means of achieving improved organizational effectiveness. In addition, the book intends to show the interaction and interdependence of the strategic planning (long and short term), detail planning, budgeting, and monitoring processes and to demonstrate how planning is an essential first step in the preparation of an effective budget for the organization.

Keywords

budgeting, business models, competitive advantage, detail planning, external analysis, forecasting, front-end strategy analysis, internal analysis, long-term planning, organizational planning systems, planning, short-term planning, situational analysis, strategic planning, strategies, strategy development

Contents

Preface

The major focus of this how-to book is to discuss and present effective planning and budgeting concepts and those related activities necessary for the successful growth of the organization. The planning process is shown to be an integral function of developing management strategies for future growth and for gaining competitive advantage in these fast-moving times. Budgeting is presented as a logical outgrowth and an essential part of the planning process rather than an independent internal activity. The emphasis is on the principal factors that should be considered in planning and budgeting for the company, what management and operations personnel must know to better understand effective planning for the business, and what can be done to enhance the overall strategic and financial planning for the organization.

Questions that will be addressed and hopefully answered to your satisfaction include the following issues and concerns:

1. What is the relationship between planning and budgeting activities?
2. What are the major elements of the strategic planning process?
3. How are short-term and detail-planning activities integrated as part of the overall planning process?
4. What are significant budgeting and profit-planning issues to consider?
5. What are some effective practices to effectively implement business strategies so that the company can be most effective and gain the competitive advantage?
6. How are management control and reporting concepts used to close the planning loop and ensure successful implementation of planning and budgeting activities?

The intent of this book is to introduce and explain the relationship between effective planning methods (long term and short term) and the budgeting and control processes. The material concentrates on practical approaches to organizational planning and integration with budgeting as well as on enhancing familiarity with related concepts and methodology. The book is designed as a how-to book for those who desire to increase their knowledge and practical use of planning and budgeting techniques as a means of achieving improved organizational effectiveness.

The purpose of the book is to show the interaction and interdependence of the strategic planning, detail planning, budgeting, and monitoring processes and to demonstrate how planning is an essential first step in the preparation of an effective budget for the organization.

The objectives of the book are

1. to increase readers' understanding of the relationship between organizational planning and the budgeting process;
2. to familiarize readers with strategic planning concepts and techniques upon which to base the budget;
3. to increase knowledge of short-term planning methodology, including organizational, departmental, and functional goal and objective setting;
4. to increase understanding of detail planning procedures, plan implementation, and related monitoring;
5. to present effective budgeting techniques that relate to the organizational planning process;
6. to increase understanding of the relationship between strategic, long-term, short-term, and detail planning and the budgeting process and the concept of flexibility to change in plans and the related activity levels of operations; and
7. to review effective planning and budgeting evaluation and control principles.

The book should not only help you to enhance your own planning and budgeting abilities, but also enable you to better serve your internal and external clients. You should, of course, exercise your own professional judgment as to which of these principles and techniques can be adapted effectively based on each specific situation. The book should be most helpful to those of you who are responsible for or significantly involved in your organization's planning activities. The degree to which you will benefit depends on a number of factors such as the size of the organization, nature of the business, number and skills of personnel applying these concepts, and the ability to match the principles covered to the specific situation. The planning and budgeting ideas and concepts discussed can be successfully implemented in any size organization.

> **A BUSINESS IS NEVER SO HEALTHY**
> **AS WHEN IT MUST PLAN FOR GROWTH**

CHAPTER 1

Internal Operational Planning Considerations

The purpose of this chapter is to identify some of the significant factors that should be in place in internal operations to ensure that the planning and budgeting process is most successful in moving the organization toward desired growth.

The objectives of this chapter are to

1. introduce some of the overarching issues that need to be addressed in internal operations to ensure that the planning and budgeting process is most successful in achieving desired results;
2. identify specific tools to enhance internal operations so that they function most economically, efficiently, and effectively;
3. introduce the concepts of best practices in a program of continuous improvements leading toward becoming a learning organization;
4. examine the various steps for analyzing and improving internal operations in an effort to support the planning and budgeting process; and
5. identify operational issues that need to be considered to make operations do the best they can to support the planning and budgeting process from strategic planning through detail plans and budgetary issues.

Introduction

We assume that all organizations plan and budget. Some do it formally, others informally or even furtively; some are effective, others ineffective, or even counterproductive in their methods. But all do it! The advantages of formalizing and throwing open the planning and budgeting process will be examined in the hope that you will recognize that an open, integrated, and reasonably structured planning and budgeting process will significantly benefit the long-term viability of the organization.

All businesses, from the very largest to the very smallest, must know where to focus their planning and budgeting efforts—organizationwide, departmental, and functional. The first step is to make all internal operations the best possible using best practices in a program of continuous improvements that makes each activity operate in the most economical, efficient, and effective manner possible. Once internal operations are running at the desired optimum level, then the organization is ready for effective planning and budgeting, always looking for opportunities to exploit their competitive advantage. Planning and budgeting activities are an integral part of the organization's growth process, and as such must be attended to actively, methodically, and effectively. Chances of success, while never ensured, will at least be significantly enhanced as a result. And to make the planning and budgeting process most successful, the organization must learn how to execute the plans and budgets—that is, to achieve desired results at the least cost.

Every organization—whether manufacturing, service provider, or not-for-profit—must plan its future direction if it desires to achieve its goals. The organizational plan is an agreed upon course of action to be implemented in the future (short and long term) and directed toward moving the entity closer to stated goals and objectives. The planning process, if exercised properly, forces the organization to

1. review and analyze past accomplishments;
2. determine present and future needs; and
3. recognize strengths and weaknesses.

And enables the organization to

1. identify future opportunities;
2. define constraints or threats that may get in the way;
3. establish business and departmental goals and objectives;
4. develop action plans based on the evaluation of alternatives; and
5. prioritize the selection of action plans for implementation based on the most effective use of limited resources.

The first step in the planning process is to determine why the organization is in existence. While many would quickly say, "To make money!" there are many other reasons, which might include:

- To provide the best quality goods or services for customers or clients
- To provide goods and services at the least cost possible
- To provide customers and clients with the best service possible
- To maintain and enhance *state-of-the-art* technological positions
- To provide employment opportunities
- To achieve personal satisfaction and gratification for the owners and employees
- To create an innovative and creative atmosphere where people can grow and develop to their full potential
- To be a productive member of the communities in which the company conducts its business and
- To be the leader in the field

> **LONG-TERM PLANNING**
> **INFERS THERE WILL BE A LONG TERM**

Why the Business Is in Existence

Before one even thinks about implementing effective planning and budgeting operating practices and controls, it is necessary to determine why a seriously operated business is in existence. When business owners and management are asked this question, invariably the answer is to make money. Although this is true and certainly important for survival and growth, there are really only two major reasons for a business to exist.

1. *The customer service business*—To provide goods and services to satisfy desired customers so that they will continue to use the business's goods and services and refer it favorably to others.

An organizational philosophy that correlates with this goal that has been found to be successful is as follows:

To provide the highest quality products and services at the least possible cost at the right time to the right customer.

2. **The cash conversion business**—To create desired goods and services so that the investment in the business is as quickly converted to cash as possible, with the resultant cash in exceeding the cash out (net profits or positive return on investment).

The correlating philosophy to this goal can be stated as follows:

To achieve desired organizational results using the most efficient methods of operations so that the organization can optimize the use of limited resources.

This means that the organization is in business to stay for the long term—to serve its customers and to grow and prosper. If they can operate under these two concepts, the possibilities for success increase and the business is more likely to expand in the right direction. Typically reporting controls emphasize sales, costs, and calculated profits. It is equally important to control the level of customer service to ensure ongoing growth as well as the ability to properly control the cash conversion cycle. The business operates on cash, not recorded profits. Proper operating practices encompassing these concepts help to ensure that the business maintains its focus and operates in the most effective manner—doing the right thing, the right way, at the right time.

**DOING THE RIGHT THING,
THE RIGHT WAY,
AT THE RIGHT TIME**

Businesses the Organization Is Not in

Once short-term thinking is eliminated, business owners and management realize they are not in the following businesses, and decision making becomes simpler.

Sales Business

Making sales that cannot be collected profitably (sales are not profits until the cash is received and the total cost of the sale is less than the amount collected) creates only numerical growth. Unless management understands this concept, they may continue to believe that increased sales create positive growth for their business. The focus is to make quality sales to quality customers. Proper operating controls over each sale as to its real profitability looking at sales price less related costs such as direct product, functional (such as purchasing, billing, and collections), customer related costs, and the cost of money should enable the business to recognize such opportunities. True customer service dictates that the business provides what the customer wants and not what the organization wants to sell.

Customer Order Backlog Business

Logging customer orders is a paperwork process to impress internal management and external stakeholders. Unless this backlog can be converted into a timely sale and profitable collection, there is only a future promise, which may never materialize. The business cannot really afford the luxury of customer backlog where every customer and every order must be handled as the only one. Once a customer order is received the business must process and fill it (and collect) in the shortest time possible. Controls need to be implemented that ensure each customer order is entered into the production system upon receipt and handled in the desired manner until completion. Working with the customer to provide products and services that the customer wants as to quality, timeliness, and price is the key to customer satisfaction and long-term satisfied relations.

Accounts Receivable Business

Get the cash as quickly as possible, not the promise to pay. But, remember, customers are the company's business; keeping them in business is keeping the company in business. Normally, cash is already out to vendors or into inventories, complicating the cash conversion process. As many businesses, such as retailers, are already in the cash business, accounts receivable are not their problem, control of cash is the problem. For those businesses that offer billing terms, consideration should be given to establish a cash only policy over small sales where the amount of the sale is less than the cost of billing and collections, and for sales under a certain amount, say $500. For instance, the business may establish controls to ensure cash collectability either in advance or at the time of delivery. All sales resulting in accounts receivable would be reported as exceptions for follow-up.

For large sales, effective customer service negotiations should be put in place to determine if the large customer would be willing to pay in advance for receiving quality and timeliness concessions, as well as favorable prices. For instance, the business may establish controls to ensure cash collectability either in advance or at the time of delivery. All sales resulting in accounts receivable would be reported as exceptions for follow-up. Working together with the customer and providing excellent customer service not only helps to reduce or eliminate accounts receivable, but also to increase ongoing business.

Inventory Business

Inventory does not equal sales. Keep inventories to a minimum—zero if possible, by procuring raw materials from vendors only as needed, producing for real customer orders based on agreed upon delivery dates, maximizing work-in-process throughput, and shipping directly from production when the customer needs the product.

To accomplish these inventory goals, it is necessary to develop an effective organizational life stream that includes the company's vendors, employees, and customers—as well as take an organizationwide approach to customer service.

If inventory is the business such as a wholesaler, retailer, or distributor, then once again the business wants to ensure that inventories are kept to a minimum within the constraints of fully serving customers. However, management must be in touch with costs and selling prices and knowing what items are in demand by the customer base. Making buying mistakes which result in selling off inventory at markdown prices is not the course to take for making the business successful. Such markdown practices usually only result in absorbing losses, setting bad precedent for customer expectations, and ignoring the root of your problems—lack of knowledge of the business and its customers.

Integrating the customer service function with the sales function allows the company to determine their inventory needs based on real customer orders rather than anticipated customer demand so that the company can

1. plan its inventory needs based on real sales and not "hoped for" sales forecast numbers imagined by the sales force;
2. minimize finished goods inventory levels by shipping directly from production or planned for finished goods stores;
3. ship directly to the customer at the time the product is needed;
4. reduce accounts receivable and its attendant processing costs by using effective customer negotiating techniques whereby the customer may be willing to pay at the time of shipment or receipt (or in advance) or in a more timely fashion—possibly reducing or eliminating the need for billing, posting of accounts receivable, and resultant collection and cash receipt procedures; and
5. revamp the sales function from one of order takers, and selling those products that maximize their commissions, to integration with the company goals as to which products to sell, in what quantities, and at what time, and to which customers and at what price.

> **THE PESSIMISTIC BUSINESS**
> **IS THE ONE WHICH WINDS UP**
> **IN THE MARK-DOWN BUSINESS**
> **HOPING TO RECOVER THROUGH VOLUME**

Property, Plant, and Equipment Business

Maintain property, plant, and equipment at a minimum, but be efficient in its use. Idle plant and equipment causes internal operational anxiety and may result in inefficient use—that is using what's there rather than letting it sit idle. If it is there, it will be used. A good suggestion is to plan for the normal (or small valleys) not for the maximum (or large peaks), network to out-source for additional capacity, and in-source for times of excess capacity. Working directly with your quality customers helps to define their present and future needs and correlates to the use and need for property, plant, and equipment.

Employment Business

The trick here is to get by with the least number of employees as possible. Never hire an additional employee unless absolutely necessary, relying on cross training and transferring good employees. Not only do people cost ongoing salaries and fringe benefits, but they also need to be paid attention to—which results in organization building. This is extremely important to any business, as smaller businesses cannot afford to solve their problems (as large corporations do) by hiring or downsizing. The business must solve similar problems with fewer employees, but more flexible. Controls over the area of personnel include hiring statistics, effective use of personnel, productivity reporting, and results produced by employee.

Management and Administrative Business

The more an organization has, more difficult it becomes to manage its business. It is easier to work with less and be able to control operations than to spend time managing the managers. So much of management becomes getting in the way of those it is supposed to manage and meeting with other managers to discuss how to do this. Management becomes the promotion for doing. Delegating authority over customer service dictates the need for fewer managers.

If an organization does both of these successfully—that is, pay attention to its business, and stay out of the businesses it should not be in—it will more than likely (outside economic factors notwithstanding) grow and prosper through well-satisfied customers and keep itself in the positive cash conversion business, in spite of itself. Management must decide which of the aforementioned factors it wishes to embrace as its business criteria, which ones it decides not to include as criteria, and which additional criteria to include. These criteria become the overriding conditions upon which the business conducts its operations, plans and budgets, and against which it is measured. It is these agreed upon criteria based on the earlier factors that define the operating practices that need to be established.

Of course, an organization also has to stay out of the numbers business, that is, looking at short-term reporting criteria: the amount of sales, backlog, locations, employees, and, the big devil, *the bottom line* that others judge as success. Effective customer service procedures implemented throughout the company ensures greater long-term growth through building rapport with quality customers (those that repetitively purchase from your company) and extracting bona fide referrals to other quality customers. This may not always be a short-term process with quick results but it is an ongoing methodology for survival and steady long-term growth.

> **EMBRACING THE CORRECT CRITERIA IS ONE ISSUE, ENFORCING THE APPLICATION OF THE CRITERIA IS ANOTHER ISSUE**

Basic Operating Formula

Many business owners, CEOs, and members of top management have some measure of success or survival through their knowledge and skills in a technical area (such as sales, retailing, engineering, auto mechanics, or etc.) but may possess minimal knowledge relative to basic good operating practices. In working with certain members of management, it is helpful to share some accounting basics that may have been learned by accountants back in Accounting 101, but these nonaccounting mangers may have never learned or comprehended. The following formula exemplifies the basic relationship between sales or revenues, costs or expenditures, and the resultant profit (or loss).

$$R - E = I$$

R = Revenues (or sales)
E = Expenditures (or costs)
I = Income

By adding an additional dollar of sales to the business, the top line increases (gross sales), but unless expenditures are less than the amount of the sale, the contribution to the profit line will be a zero or less (i.e., a negative or loss). However, by reducing expenditures by a dollar (all other things being equal), the reduction will fall directly to the bottom line and increase profits on a dollar-by-dollar basis. Accordingly, business success is dependent upon business management acquiring only quality sales from quality customers (i.e., those sales that contribute a desired profit to the bottom line, and the maintaining of costs at a minimum. Of course, business management must be aware of their costs and related pricing structure for each of its products and services and customers.

**AN INCREASE IN SALES MAY CREATE A LOSS,
A DECREASE IN COSTS CREATES A GAIN IN INCOME**

Helpful Systems

In many businesses today, management is grasping for ways to become competitive and maintain market position—or merely to survive. The owners and management have sensed that many of their systems are detrimental to growth and have held them back. These are the very systems that are supposed to be helpful. For example:

1. Planning systems, long and short term, that resulted in formal or informal plans but not in actual results.
2. Budget systems that became costly in terms of allocating resources effectively and controlling costs in relation to results.
3. Organizational structures that created unwieldy hierarchies or gaps in responsibilities, which produced systems of unnecessary policing and control.
4. Cost accounting structures (usually lack thereof) that obscured true product costs and resulted in pricing that constrained competitiveness or ignored profitability.
5. Computerized accounting systems that produced elaborate reporting without enhancing the effectiveness of operations.

6. Sales functions and forecasts that resulted in selling those products that maximized sales commissions but may not have been the products to sell and produce for effective growth.

Operating practices that perpetuate outmoded systems ("we've always done it that way") rather than promote best practices are a dominant factor in perpetuating the causes that sabotage making and maintaining these helpful systems more ineffectual. Effective operating practices that ensure that these systems are operating most effectively, together with other techniques, are tools to make these systems helpful as intended and direct the organization toward its goals. With the passage of time, good intentions and, initially, helpful systems tend to deteriorate. Operational reviews are then necessary to help get the business back on track by pinpointing operational deficiencies, developing practical recommendations, and implementing positive changes. In most cases, an encompassing effective operational review is required prior to developing any long or short term plans and related budgets.

> **HELPFUL SYSTEMS**
> **ARE MEANT TO BE HELPFUL**

Business Success Formula

The business needs to understand the relationship between obtaining a customer sales order and the flow within the business that results ultimately in a positive profit. This process is described in the following business success formula:

$$CO = BL = PO = SR + AR = CR - TC = GP$$

CO = Customer Order

Each customer sales order must be entered into the business records as soon as it is a reality. For major customers, the business's goal is to obtain long-term negotiated commitments from these customers so that the business can plan its providing of products or services in advance. Ideally for manufacturers such negotiated commitments can be automatically plugged into their production schedule. In addition, the business should attempt to get as much cash advance up front as possible—100 percent for agreed upon small purchases.

BL = Backlog Order

If the business cannot immediately enter and process the customer's sale order, it becomes backlog—that is, a bona fide sales order that cannot be processed. Ideally, backlog should be zero. If a sales order must be entered into backlog, it is an indication that the business is not operating effectively.

PO = Production Order

If the business does not have the items ordered on site or in inventory, then the order must be processed internally and entered into the system as a production order, or order in process. The PO should not be entered into production any earlier than necessary to ensure timely shipment to the customer. The operating controls from this point are to produce the order as quickly as possible using facilities efficiently so that all customer orders are completed to meet customer shipment requirements.

SR + AR = Sale Recording + Accounts Receivable

If the business has not received a cash payment in advance or at the time of shipment, the customer will have to be billed and the sale is set up as an accounts receivable. At this point, the customer has the materials and the business has a bill to the customer with payment terms—which may or may not be honored. Accordingly, it is incumbent upon the business to get out of the accounts receivable business where possible and ensure that all bills are paid in a timely fashion—in advance if possible or at time of shipment or providing of services.

CR − TC = Cash Receipts − Total Costs

The cash receipt should be received by the business as quickly as possible— hopefully prior to shipping or providing the product. However, where billing and collections must be done the business must be vigilant in collecting the cash payment as quickly as possible. Note that, if discounts are offered for early payment, such cost must be calculated as part of total costs. A good rule is to set prices after deducting for the offered discount, resulting in getting the desired price from those customers paying within the discount terms and penalizing those others by the amount of the discount for late payment. In addition, the cost of money for the period of collection must be considered as part of total costs. Other costs accumulated as part of total costs include direct product or service costs (e.g., material and labor), indirect costs associated with the product or service (e.g., quality control, receiving, and shipping), functional costs (e.g., sales, marketing, engineering, and accounting), and customer costs (e.g., presales contacts, during sales contacts, and after sales contacts).

GP = Gross Profit

Theoretically, each customer and each sale to that customer can be looked at as a profit center. If the business follows this formula, each sale can be controlled as to its contribution to gross profits, and any necessary remedial action can be taken at the time of the transaction.

**EACH CUSTOMER
AND EACH CUSTOMER SALE
IS A PROFIT CENTER**

Management Responsibility

Managers at all levels should be held accountable for using the scarce resources entrusted to them to achieve maximum results at the least possible costs. Although management should embrace best practice operating concepts and apply them as they proceed, in the typical business this is rarely the case.

More normally, business management needs to be sold on the value of differential systems. In selling the benefits of implementing such operating practices, it is important to stress that unlike other techniques that cost time and money for uncertain results, best operating practices can pay for themselves. In effect, the operations and control environment becomes a profit center instead of a cost center.

With the success of best practice operating procedures, management quickly realizes that the more the effective operating practices are in place and the more the recommended economies and efficiencies are implemented, the greater the savings and results. In addition, the residual capability for implementing and performing best practice operating procedures remains in each operating area, so that operations personnel can continue to apply these concepts on an ongoing basis.

Keep in mind that the intent of implementing best practice operating procedures is not to be critical of present operations, but to review operations and develop a program of best practices and continuous positive operational improvements by working with management and staff personnel. The concept of best practices should be sold as an internal program of review directed toward improved economies and efficiencies that will produce increased operational results. With best operating practices in place, success of planning and budgeting procedures is greatly enhanced.

**THE SUCCESSFUL BUSINESS
IS THE ONE THAT LISTENS AND TRIES
ALTERNATIVE APPROACHES
LOOKING FOR THE PATH TO SUCCESS**

Some Basic Business Principles

Once the business has defined the reason(s) for its existence and its purpose, management must define the basic business principles upon which they desire to operate the business and to have it function. As business owners and management, they have the right to define whatever business principles they desire and to expect their employees to follow such principles. However, the definition of such business principles provides clear communication to all employees (and vendors and customers) as to how the business is to operate. Each business must determine the specific basic principles upon which it conducts its operations. These principles become the foundation that the business bases its plans and budgets and desirable operations and results.

Examples of such business principles include the following:

- Produce the best quality product at the least possible cost.
- Set selling prices realistically, so as to sell the entire product that can be produced within the constraints of the production facilities.
- Build trusting relationships with critical vendors; keeping them in business is keeping the company in business.
- The company is in the customer service and cash conversion businesses.
- Don't spend a dollar that doesn't need to be spent; a dollar not spent is a dollar to the bottom line. Control costs effectively; there is more to be made here, than increased sales.
- Manage the company; do not let it manage the managers. Provide guidance and direction, not crises.
- Identify the company's customers and develop marketing and sales plans with the customers in mind. Produce for the company's customers, not for inventory. Serve the customers, not sell them.
- Don't hire employees unless they are absolutely needed, and only when they multiply the company's effectiveness, so that the company makes more from them than if they did it themselves.
- Keep property, plant, and equipment to the minimum necessary for customer demand.
- Plan for the realistic, but develop contingency plans for the positive unexpected.

With sensible business principles, the business can be clear as to the direction for positive movement and avoid merely improving poor practices. Clear business principles that make sense to all levels of the organization allow the business to identify and develop the proper operational practices. In this manner, everyone in the organization is moving in the same desired direction—singing out of the same songbook.

> **MANAGEMENT CAN DO IT THEIR WAY—OR THE RIGHT WAY**

Mental Models and Belief Systems

Many businesses operate on the basis of prevalent mental models or belief systems— usually emanating from present (and past) owners and management. These mental models have an overriding effect on the conditions with which operations within the business are carried out. They can help to produce a helpful working environment, or atmosphere, or a hindering one. In effect, such mental models become performance drivers—those elements within the business that shape the direction of how employees perform their functions. Examples include the following:

1. The obedient child in the company survives and is promoted, while the rebellious child is let go or leaves the company.
2. Only owners or managers can make decisions.
3. Power rises to the top—and stays there.
4. Employees need to be watched for them to do their jobs.
5. Power and control over employees is necessary to get results.
6. Owners or managers are responsible, employees are basically irresponsible.
7. Those at the top of the organization know what they are doing.
8. All functions should be organized in the same manner.
9. Higher levels of organization are needed to ensure that lower levels do their jobs.
10. Policing and control over employees is needed to ensure their compliance.
11. All employees are interchangeable.
12. Doing the job right is more important than doing the right job.
13. Control people, control results.
14. Organizational position is more important than being right.
15. Owners or management has the right to set all policies and procedures.
16. Owners or managers create results—employees do the job.

17. Organizational hierarchies are needed to ensure that things get done.
18. Employees cannot be trusted on their own.
19. You cannot run a business without the proper organizational structure.
20. Owners or managers know more than employees.
21. Owners or managers have a right to be obnoxious.
22. Owners or management is the enemy.
23. Each function needs its own organizational structure.
24. The more employees reporting to you (and the larger your budget), the more important you are within the organization.

The accurate identification of organizational mental models, belief systems, and performance drivers is extremely important in analyzing the business's operations. If these things are not changed, operational changes will only change the system and not business results. With the best plans and budgets, results will be minimized with the wrong mental models in place.

CHANGE THE MENTAL MODEL, INCREASE PLANNING RESULTS—IF YOU BELIEVE IT THEN IT IS SO

Operating Areas to Be Addressed

While typically managements' major concern is daily operations, to be most effective, one must include any and all organizational functions and activities that hinder or help the effort to maintain the business in the most economical, efficient, and effective manner possible. In this regard, you must be aware of basic business principles that help to enhance the organization's success as well as those that the company should avoid. With these principles in mind, the business's operations can be analyzed to identify areas for improvement in which best practices can be implemented that maximize the chances of planning success and minimize the risk of failure. Although the primary focus in identifying and establishing these operating practices is in the manner in which scarce resources are used, considering the sources and uses of resources and the policies and procedures used to deal with the over and under operational conditions, these are specific areas that need to be addressed.

The first step in successfully identifying and implementing effective business operating practices is to define the company's desired criteria for results as related to their reasons for existence and basic business principles. These organizational criteria typically encompass the company as an entity as well as its major functions. Such criteria then become the basis for establishing plans and budgetary controls to monitor progress toward it. An example of such an organizationwide criteria structure is as follows:

- Operate all activities in the most economical, efficient, and effective manner as possible.
- Provide the highest quality products to customers at the least possible cost.
- Satisfy customers so that they continue to use the company's products and refer the company to others.
- Convert the cash invested in the business as quickly as possible so that the resultant cash in exceeds the cash out to the greatest extent possible.
- Achieve desired results using the most efficient methods so that the company can optimize the use of limited resources.
- Maximize net profits without sacrificing quality of operations, customer service, or cash requirements.

> **IF YOU KEEP YOUR EYE ONLY ON THE OPERATIONS, YOU'LL MISS THE RESULTS**

Based on these established organizationwide criteria, the business can then establish related criteria for the major areas of operations such as the following.

Sales Function

In the best of circumstances, the criterion for the most effective and efficient sales operation involves making sales to the right customers who provide a profit source to the business. A strong sales function creates realistic sales forecasts that result in a present or future real customer order. Sales orders and corresponding compensation systems should reinforce the goals of the company; that is, what items to sell, how much of each item to sell, at what price, and to whom. And finally, customer sales should be integrated with other functions of the company, such as manufacturing, engineering, accounting, purchasing, and so on. Some questions to ask in the planning process include:

- Are sales made to quality customers with the right products at the right time?
- Does each sale make a contribution to profits?
- Are all costs compared to the sale such as product costs (direct material and labor), assignment of product related activity costs (e.g., manufacturing processes, quality control, shipping, and receiving), functional costs (e.g., purchasing, accounts payable, billing, and accounts receivable), and customer costs (e.g., marketing, selling, support services, and customer service)?
- Do sales relate to an agreed upon sales forecast? Is the company selling the right products to the right customers?
- Do sales integrate with an effective production scheduling or control system?
- Are sales made to the right customers that can be collected profitably?
- Do realistic sales forecast result in a present or future real customer order?
- Are sales for those products, as determined by management, sold to the right customers, at the right time, and in the right quantities?
- Do actual customer sales correlate directly with management's long- and short-term plans?
- Do sales efforts and corresponding compensation systems reinforce the goals of the company?
- Are customer sales integrated with other functions of the company, such as manufacturing, engineering, accounting, purchasing, and so on.

Direct Cost

The business wants to operate in the most efficient manner with the most economical cost in the timeliest manner, considering processes such as customer order entry, production and service delivery throughput, and customer delivery. The business should integrate manufacturing and service delivery processes with sales efforts and customer requirements, and increase productivity of manufacturing and service delivery operations on an ongoing basis. Direct cost control goals should include eliminating, reducing, and improving all facets of the business's operations, especially those nonvalue-added costs, including activities such as receiving, inventory control, production control, storeroom operations, quality control, supervision and management, packing and shipping, and maintenance. The business should also be concerned with minimizing the amount of resources such as personnel, facilities, and equipment that are allocated to the manufacturing or service delivery process. Planning questions to ask include:

- Are sales orders entered into an effective production control system, which ensures that all sales orders are entered into production in a timely manner to ensure on time, quality deliveries?
- Is work-in-process kept to a minimum so that only real customer orders are being worked on rather than building up finished goods inventory?
- Are the most efficient and economical production methods used to ensure that the cost of the product is kept to its realizable minimum?
- Are direct materials and labor used most efficiently so that waste, reworks, and rejects are kept to a minimum?
- Are nondirect labor (and material) costs such as quality control, supervision and management, repairs and maintenance, material handling, and so on kept to a minimum?
- Are all operations conducted in the most efficient manner with the most economical costs?

- Are manufacturing and service delivery processes integrated with sales efforts and customer requirements?
- Are manufacturing and service delivery operations conducted in the timeliest manner considering processes such as customer order entry, timely throughput, and customer delivery?
- Is there a system in effect to increase productivity in all operations on an ongoing basis?
- Are controls in effect to eliminate, reduce, or improve all facets of business operations?
- Do procedures exist to eliminate, reduce, or improve all facets of manufacturing and service delivery operations?
- Are resources minimized such as personnel, facilities, and equipment that are allocated to the manufacturing or service delivery process?
- Are raw materials and finished goods inventories kept to a minimum?
- Are raw materials delivered into production on a just-in-time basis?
- Are finished goods completed in production just in time for customer delivery?
- Is the business working toward getting out of the inventory business?

Functional Activities

While the emphasis for many businesses is to continually increase sales, it is the responsibility of management to obtain profitable sales from quality customers, convert a sale into cash as quickly as possible, and add real profits to the bottom line—more important components in operating a successful business. Many times the business cannot control the acquisition of customer sales when needed, resulting, sometimes, in making a sale for less than a desired profit margin (possibly at a loss). However, the business can initiate efforts to control and reduce its internal functional costs, resulting in an increase in its profit margins, and creating greater flexibility in its pricing policies. Remember a dollar of cost saved is a dollar that goes directly to the bottom line. Some of the areas of concern for typical functional costs are as follows.

Accounting Functions—General

- What is the purpose and necessity of each of the accounting functions and related activities, such as accounts receivable, accounts payable, payroll, budgeting, and general ledger?
- Is each of the accounting functions operated in the most economical and efficient manner?
- Are effective procedures in effect that result in the accounting functions becoming more analytical than mechanical?
- Are computerized procedures developed that integrate accounting purposes with operating requirements?
- Do reporting systems exist that provide management with the necessary operating data and indicators that can be generated from accounting data?
- Is there a process that identifies, eliminates, or reduces all unnecessary accounting operations?

Billing, Accounts Receivable, and Collections

- Are bills sent out in a timely manner—at the time of shipment or before?
- Are accounts receivable processing procedures the most efficient and economical?
- Is the cost of billing, accounts receivable processing, and collection efforts more costly than the amount of the receivable or the net profit on the sale?
- Is the number and amount of accounts receivable continually analyzed for minimization?
- Are any customers paying directly or through electronic funds transfer at the time of shipping or delivery?
- Are bills and accounts receivable in amounts exceeding the cost of processing excluded from the system?

Purchasing and Accounts Payable

- Are all items that are less than the cost of purchasing excluded from the purchasing system—with an efficient system used for these items?
- Is all repetitive high volume and cost items (e.g., raw materials and manufacturing supplies) negotiated, by purchasing, with vendors as to the price, quality, and timeliness?
- Does the production system automatically order repetitive items as an integrated part of the production control system?
- Has consideration been given to reduce these functions for low- and high-ticket items leading toward the possible elimination of these functions?
- Does the company consider paying any vendors on a shipment or delivery basis as part of its vendor negotiation procedures?
- Does the purchasing function only purchase those items where economies can be gained through a system of central purchasing?
- Is there a direct purchase system for those items that the purchasing function does not need to process, such as low dollar purchases and repetitive purchases?
- Are purchasing and accounts payable systems simplified so that costs are at the lowest possible levels?
- Do purchasing personnel effectively negotiate with vendors so that the company obtains the right materials at the right time, at the right quality, and at the right price?
- Is there a vendor analysis system present that objectively evaluates vendor performance?

Other Costs and Expenses

- Are all other costs and expenses kept to a minimum? Remember, an unnecessary dollar not spent is a dollar directly to the bottom line.
- Are selling costs directed toward customer service and strategic plans rather than maximizing sales people's compensation?

- Is there a system in effect which recognizes and rewards the reduction of expenses rather than budget increases or increased expenditures?
- Are all nonvalue-added functions (e.g., management and supervision, office processing, paperwork, and so on) evaluated as to reduction and elimination?

**IF YOU DON'T KNOW WHERE YOU'RE GOING
AND THE RESULTS TO BE ACHIEVED
THERE IS NOTHING TO CONTROL AGAINST**

Economy, Efficiency, and Effectiveness

In establishing effective operating practices for business success and to make the planning and budgeting process more successful, such practices must embrace the concept of conducting operations for economy, efficiency, and effectiveness. The following is a brief description of each of the three Es of effective operations.

Economy (or The Cost of Operations)

Is the business carrying out its responsibilities in the most economical manner—that is, through due conservation of its resources? In appraising the economy of operations and related allocation and use of resources, you may consider whether the organization is

- following sound purchasing practices;
- overstaffed as related to performing necessary functions;
- allowing excess materials to be on hand;
- using equipment that is more expensive than necessary;
- avoiding the wastage of resources.

Efficiency (or Methods of Operations)

Is the organization carrying out its responsibilities with the minimum expenditure of effort? Examples of operational inefficiencies to be aware of include:

- improper use of manual and computerized procedures;
- inefficient paperwork flow;
- inefficient operating systems and procedures;
- cumbersome organizational hierarchy or communication patterns;
- duplication of effort;
- unnecessary work steps.

Effectiveness (or Results of Operations)

Is the organization achieving results or benefits based on stated goals and objectives or some other measurable criteria? The review of the results of operations includes the

- appraisal of the organizational planning system as to its development of realistic goals, objectives, and detail plans;
- assessment of the adequacy of management's system for measuring effectiveness;
- determination of the extent to which results are achieved; and
- identification of factors inhibiting satisfactory performance of results.

A graphic way to look at the effect of economy, efficiency, and effectiveness on the business's growth and profitability is shown in the following formula.

ECONOMY, EFFICIENCY, AND EFFECTIVENESS FORMULA FOR GROWTH

$$G + P = E1 + E2 + E3$$

G = Growth
P = Profitability
$E1$ = Economy
$E2$ = Efficiency
$E3$ = Effectiveness

For the business to be successful and grow and prosper in a profitable manner, management must operate the business using the least amount of scarce resources (economy), using sound business practices in their operations (efficiency), to achieve the optimum results of success (effectiveness).

Adequate Operating Practices

Are present if management has planned, designed, and organized in a manner that provides reasonable assurance that the organization's risks have been managed effectively, and the organization's goals and objectives will be achieved efficiently and economically producing desired results.

Organizational Planning Systems

Organizational planning systems are developed as a collaborative effort between top management and all the operating functions of the organization. This is an attempt to get all the various functions of the company working toward the same goals and objectives. The initial concern is to develop more sophisticated procedures to plan and control the company's direction, both in the long and short term. The major goals of an integrated planning system include the following:

1. Deliver high-quality products
   - Exceed customer expectations, resulting in customer satisfaction
   - Bring quality products to market faster
   - Improve quality on an ongoing basis
2. Reduce costs
   - Direct material and labor and indirect costs
   - Inventory and carrying costs
   - Quality control costs, but not quality
   - Eliminate time waste
   - Reduce defects, rework, scrap

As planning needs are defined, it is apparent that all functions need to work together. To develop an effective organizational plan, various factors must be considered, such as the following:

- The starting point for organizational planning should be the organizational operating practices—hopefully operating with best practices most economically, efficiently, and effectively.
- The nature of the business, type of manufacturing or service provided, relations with vendors and customers, operating processes, products or services to be produced, and so forth.
- What businesses the company should be in, what products or services it should be selling, to whom, and to what extent.
- The control and feedback features required for managing and controlling operations so as to meet commitments.
- Reporting requirements that enable the organization to operate in the most economical, efficient, and effective manner.

> **AN EFFECTIVE AND SUCCESSFUL PLAN**
> **REQUIRES AN EFFECTIVE ORGANIZATION**
> **AND BEST PRACTICE OPERATIONS**

Sales and Market Forecasts

The starting point in the organizational planning process is the sales and market forecast (both short-term and long-term forecasts). This is the definition of what goods and services the company desires to sell and to whom. However, because the effectiveness of the organizational plan is dependent on the accuracy of such a market or sales forecast, many companies experience planning problems before going any further, a result of their having sales forecasts that are more fiction than reality. So for most companies the first step in effective planning is to work toward more accurate sales forecasts on which to base their plans. A good rule of thumb is that an effective sales forecast should consist of at least 80 percent real customer orders. This means that the sales function will have to do the one thing they have not done in years—service the customer.

SELL WHAT THE CUSTOMER NEEDS, NOT WHAT YOU WANT TO SELL

The organization, together with the sales function, must determine what products or services (or product lines) it wishes to sell in the coming period. This decision is made by analyzing past sales, customer (and noncustomer) needs and desires, inventory levels, production and service delivery capabilities, futuristic considerations, competitive factors, and so on. An example of such a product analysis is shown in the following. Based on the analysis of these three products (or product lines), the company has to determine what it wants to do with these products in the future (see Table 1.1).

Based on the analysis of these three products (or product lines), management needs to determine what they want to do with these products in the future. For, instance, product A is a low cost or selling price item with low profit margins. Management might question whether they want to stay in this business for competitive reasons—that is, making a low cost alternative available for those customers where low price is a strong consideration—or to get out of this part of the business altogether. The company is not only achieving an unacceptable level of return, but it is also tying up resources (facilities and personnel) to be used more effectively with other products.

Table 1.1 Product Determination

Prod	SP ($)	Cost ($)	GP ($)	%[a]	Fore	Sales	Sales ($)	%[b]	Total ($)	GP (%)
A	18	15	3	16.7	800	540	9,720	2.2	1,620	1
B	32	20	12	37.5	12,000	9,800	313,600	70.2	117,600	67
C	56	30	26	46.4	3,600	2,200	123,200	27.6	57,200	32
					16,400	12,540	446,520	100.0	176,420	100

[a] % of gross profit to selling price.

[b] % of product sales to total sales.

Prod = product, SP = selling price, Cost = cost of product, GP = gross profit, Fore = sales forecast, Sales = annual sales in units, Sales $ = annual sales in dollars, Total = total gross profit contribution by product, GP % = gross profit % of each product.

Product B is the company's bread and butter product—that is, the company sells these items repetitively at a more than acceptable profit level (37.5 percent). Sales of these items account for over 70 percent the company's total business and 67 percent of gross profits. These are the items that the business is geared up for and where the sales function can easily obtain customer commitments. This is the part of the company's sales forecast that needs to be accurate. With minimal effort by sales personnel, this can be achieved—if sales personnel would only talk to the customers.

Product C is the high-price, top-of-the-line product for those customers who are willing to pay more for a luxurious look or additional options—many times a status rather than price consideration. While the company sells less of these items than product B, the profits (and usually sales commissions) are greater. Accordingly, there is a tendency for sales personnel to spend more time selling Cs than Bs, which may be counter to the company's plans—that is to sell more Bs than Cs.

Typically, the company doesn't know what their real costs (and added costs) are for such top-of-the-line items, and what internal strife this causes in producing and delivering their standard B items. Company management needs to consider their plans for product C—that is, to increase this business segment, de-emphasize it, or maintain it approximately at the current level. Management might also consider making the product C business segment a separate entity or business division. In whatever case, management must direct the sales function so that their efforts are expended where desired to meet management's plans.

**ALL BUSINESSES ARE IN A
NUMBER OF BUSINESSES**

The Arc of a Successful Product

When the business finds a product with high demand and a good profit margin (sometimes identified as a cash cow), management must be aware of such a condition to take full competitive advantage in its planning process. The arc of a successful product is shown in Figure 1.1.

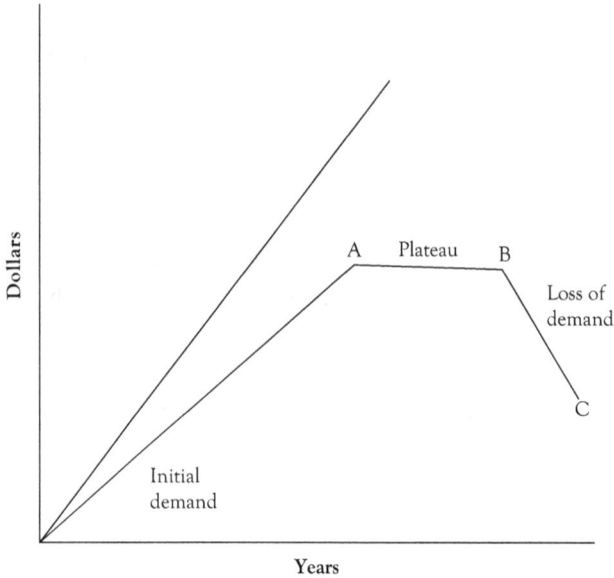

A = First point of innovation
    Competitors have come in and sales have plateaued

B = Second point of innovation
    Market has settled and total sales are decreasing

C = Point of retrenchment
    Get out of business or re-innovate

Figure 1.1 Arc of a successful product

While such a product allows management to take advantage of the marketplace by establishing an unrealistic pricing strategy, it is asking for two things to happen:

1. The market settles after all of those customers who demand or need to have the product have saturated the marketplace. Typically within a relatively short period of time, usually within a year, 80 percent of all customers who demand the product have purchased the product. After such saturation, sales will tend to plateau, and the cost to continue to increase sales at the same price becomes more costly— sometimes resulting in losses in each sale. A reduction in price may increase sales but lose the loyalty of customers who purchased the product at its high initial pricing.

2. Competitors have entered the market and absorbed market share by reducing prices and increasing quality and more reliable delivery and customer support. It is at this point that the business must decide in its planning process what to do with these products—innovate, expand marketing and sales efforts, or retrench and look for the next cash cow. This is grist for the planning process.

THE EARLY BIRD CATCHES THE WORM,
BUT THE SECOND MOUSE GETS THE CHEESE

There are many examples of the early bird and the second mouse. A few examples are given in Table 1.2.

As can be seen, some of these companies were able to have a great cash harvest as early birds and others have done quite well as the second mouse. As part of the planning process you need to look at where your products are at this point in their life arc, the position of your competition regarding these products, and whether you want to devote time, effort, and expense in becoming the early bird or to watch your competitors closely and then jump in as a second mouse—or stay out of this arena entirely—allocating your resources elsewhere.

Table 1.2 Examples of the Early Bird and the Second Mouse

Product or service	Early bird	Second mouse
Copy machine	Xerox	Canon and Sharp
PC	IBM	Compaq, Dell
Search engine	Yahoo	Google
Social network	MySpace	Facebook
Television	RCA	Philco, Zenith, etc.
Personal assistant	Palm	Blackberry
Credit card	American Express	Visa, Master Card
Smartphone	Apple	Samsung, Google, Motorola, etc.

Business Models

Business strategies that may be dependent upon the type of business the company is in, many times dictates and defines a specific business model upon which the business operates its business activities. For instance, business models of pay first (in whole or partial payment), and then provide the goods or services afterwards or a business model of *knock your socks off* customer services. Following are examples of nationally known business models related to strategic thrusts:

- *Quality differentiation*: Maytag appliances and Michelin tires
- *Low cost, minimal frills*: Walmart and Target stores, Kia automobiles, Southwest Airlines
- *Discount clothing stores (focus)*: Ross for Less, TJ Maxx
- *Customer service focus*: Old IBM, more recent Dell; Caterpillar farm equipment; office supply catalog or internet companies (Quill, the old Viking)
- *Technological position (preemption)*: Microsoft operating systems (Windows and Vista), Apple iPod, RIM Blackberry
- *Owner or employee satisfaction and gratification*: Old Ben and Jerry, Tom's Toothpaste, alternative energy
- *Innovation and creativity*: Apple, Cisco systems, software development and video game companies, and computer animation
- *Synergy*: Office Depot and Gateway, AT&T and Cingular, Johnson & Johnson and McNeil Labs (Tylenol), Adobe and Macromedia
- *Stock brokers focus*: Charles Schwab, E-Trade as opposed to Smith Barney and Merrill Lynch
- *Internet preemption*: eBay, Google, Amazon, Priceline
- *Outsourcing*: electronic manufacturing (Solectron, Flextronics), call centers (First Data, Dubai India)
- *Food service*: fast food (McDonalds, Burger King, Taco Bell, Pizza Hut), restaurant chains (Olive Garden, Chang's, TGIF, Applebee's, Cracker Barrel)

- *Brand recognition and preemption*: Starbucks coffee, Polo and Chaps clothing, Nike athletic gear
- *High-end status*: Mercedes, BMW, Lexus, Range Rover, Jenn-Air, Sub Zero

It is important to understand the various existing business models so that you can take the best advantage of their strengths and be able to avoid or remediate their weaknesses. And remember it is the second mouse that gets the cheese. As some of you may be starting, or are conducting in whole or in part, a local business, it is also a good procedure to analyze the business models of those businesses operating in your local area—which models seem to be successful and which are not. Keep in mind that you may be competing with these local businesses, but that those national concerns are also your competition and may be more formidable competitors.

**IT IS ONLY A MODEL,
UNTIL YOU GET IT TO WORK**

Front-End Strategy Analysis

In developing specific strategies for an individual business, unique characteristics and qualities relevant to the business's operations must be identified as discussed earlier. This normally requires some front-end analysis to determine exactly what strategies will be most effective. Some factors to consider relative to developing specific strategies include the following:

- **Market orientation:** The business's awareness of its external environment, including customers, competitors, and the marketplace. The goal here is to develop customer sensitive strategies that utilize the business's market strengths.
- **Proactivity:** Attempting to influence events in the environment as opposed to merely reacting to forces as they occur. Examples are lobbying for changes to a law that will significantly affect the business or trying to exploit a situation that

at first glance appears to have totally negative implications (e.g., providing environmental cleanup, toxic waste disposal, or waste management services).

- **Information systems:** The identification of existing information systems and their capability to provide accurate and timely data to make the strategy development process operate effectively. This includes the determination of what information is required, how to provide it, and the processing and analysis requirements. Another factor to consider is the ability to provide online data so that strategic changes can be made more responsively.

- **Entrepreneurial style:** Emphasizes the business's need to be more responsive to opportunities and not let an unwieldy management system bog down the decision-making process. Creating flexibility in the use of employees and delegating authority and commensurate responsibilities to the lowest level possible many times creates that competitive advantage. Business is the sum of its personnel—use them wisely.

- **Multiple strategies:** Use of multiple strategies rather than a single strategy with related financial projections may help in the development of the most effective overall strategy. The focus, however, should be on the strategy development and not on the financial projections. There are many ways to skin the competitive cat, look for the ones that will work best in your situation.

- **Implementation capability:** While proper strategy development is extremely important, it provides no more than a theoretical set of alternatives unless they can be implemented. For the process to work, the strategy must first fit the business's needs and opportunities and then must be capable of being implemented effectively.

THE STRATEGY MUST FIT
THE BUSINESS'S NEEDS
FOR IT TO WORK

Organizing the Business

Theoretically, businesses are put together so that the business can conduct its operations more efficiently and that the owners and top management can multiple their effectiveness—that is, maximize desired results. Organizing is intended to be a helping process to enable a business to conduct its business better. However, for many businesses it has become a costly getting in the way process. As part of its cost reduction analysis, the business ascertains if the organization is properly organized or if improper organization is the cause of its problems and a critical factor in excessive costs.

Adequate organizational and management control requires that each employee know clearly what his or her role and function is in the business, and exactly what *responsibilities and authority* have been assigned. It also requires proper separation of duties, an important internal control, so that the same individual is not charged with the responsibility for recording as well as reporting on how a particular task or result has been accomplished.

**ADD EMPLOYEES ONLY
TO MULTIPLY THE COMPANY'S EFFECTIVENESS**

The organization of the business should follow the principles of proper organization, which apply to any size organization, which include:

- Clear lines of authority
- Proper division of duties and responsibilities
- Communication between functions and across functions—both upward and downward
- Minimal use of personnel and then only as needed
- Proper delegation of responsibilities and authority
- Management able to effectively control the sphere of their operations and results
- Management and other personnel clearly understand what is expected of them and the results to be achieved
- Organization established based on the principles of the three Es—economy, efficiency, and effectiveness

- The right size organization for what needs to be accomplished—neither under or over staffed—like the Goldilocks principle, it should be just right
- Minimum levels of no value-added employees and management, and
- Organization no larger than it has to be to accomplish results.

Even management should understand the aforementioned principles of proper organization, normally one of two situations are bound to arise:

1. Hiring an individual for each function, just like the big boys, so that management can be surrounded with a large staff to order about and control—quite, an unnecessary cost. Sometimes even with such an organization, rather than results being accomplished, it results in employees, including management, getting in everyone's way.

MORE EMPLOYEES DO NOT ALWAYS
PRODUCE GREATER RESULTS

---

2. Hiring insufficient and incapable personnel (sometimes untrainable) to keep costs to a minimum—resulting in management doing more than necessary and running around dealing with one crisis after another. Such a situation does allow management to blame the situation on the employees—what could anyone accomplish with these bozos. This is another instance of fixing the blame rather than the cause, which is improper organization with insufficient, capable personnel.

IT'S NOT THE NUMBER OF EMPLOYEES,
IT'S HAVING THE RIGHT EMPLOYEES

Conclusion

It's not easy to know the answer as to how to organize the business. In the beginning, management might be alone as they start the business and follow their dream. Or you might be overly fearful and lonely and bring others, like a partner, into the business, too soon or unnecessarily. When starting the business and not being sure the best way to get started, it is always best to seek advice, paid or not, from those who have been through the process, hopefully with success. While it is difficult to take advice from others, as you believe you know more than them, learn to listen. It is better to start off right than to be sorry, and then having to blame those providing the advice rather than yourself.

WHEN I NEED THE EXPERIENCE,
I HAVEN'T HAD IT YET

Once the organization has identified the substantive reasons why it is in existence and has articulated them into basic business principles and best practice operating procedures, the next step is to define related business goals—both long and short term. Top management normally formulates these goals, although it is generally good practice to obtain feedback from lower level managers, supervisors, and operating personnel as to the appropriateness, practicality, reasonableness, and attainability of the goals. A good rule to keep in mind in the development of an effective organizational plan is that it is the employees closest to day-to-day operations who usually know the most about present problems, and what needs to be done to correct them. Accordingly, it is imperative for the business that wishes to be successful over the long term to have representatives from many levels in the organization involved throughout the planning process. Many companies have been unsuccessful in their planning efforts and their ability to survive because of lack of foresight, and their inability to use employee input creatively—and ineffective internal operating practices.

In addition, operating personnel need to know how to plan properly and operate according to the plans in order to conduct their operations successfully in an integrated and coordinated way. Operating personnel cannot plan for their own areas effectively unless they understand the organization's long- and short-term goals, and have had the opportunity to provide significant input and feedback to these plans. It is not sufficient that operations personnel be allowed merely to provide input and feedback; top management must actively encourage their input and seriously consider it in the finalization of goals. The development of organizational goals must be institutionalized as a system of top to bottom involvement for it to be maximally successful.

On the other hand, we must understand that top management has the ultimate decision-making power and therefore may still decide to do whatever they wish, regardless of operations personnel input. The result of such exclusive top management decision-making, however, is goal setting by directive rather than by participation. Operations staff will see the goals as top management's and not their own, and they will not only be less inclined to direct efforts toward their achievement, but may work openly against or even sabotage their accomplishment. In an effective planning system, it is extremely important to have everyone in the organization working toward the same goals. In this manner, management and operations staff is far more likely to make decisions that are consistent with the company's overall direction.

Within this framework, how then does an organization plan effectively for its future? Note that in the development of long-range plans down to the development of detail plans and related budgets, there should be a top-to-bottom approach used, wherein top management and operating personnel interact and communicate. This results in a coordinated and agreed-upon set of company and departmental objectives, plans, and budgets.

CHAPTER 2

Strategic (Long-Range) Planning

The purpose of this chapter is to review the strategic planning process for an organization with the idea of introducing the concepts, steps, issues, and other considerations that must be taken into account in carrying out this activity. Also, to identify some of the significant factors in the planning and budgeting processes that needs to be examined, and to look at the relationship of budgeting to the overall strategic planning process for the organization.

The objectives of this chapter are to

1. identify the basic elements of strategic planning;
2. articulate some fundamental strategies a company may wish to consider;
3. examine the steps involved in the strategic planning process; and
4. introduce some tools that can help make the process easier and more effective for the organization.

**THE PRESENT AND THE PAST
AFFECT THE FUTURE**

Overview to Strategic Planning

The process of developing and implementing strategies has been in existence for a number of years and has been referred to by numerous terms such as strategic planning, strategic management, long-range planning, and budgeting and control. The development of these *budgeting and control management systems* can be traced back to the early 1900s. The emphasis then was on controlling deviations from established budgets and attempting to simplify the management of divergent areas of the organization. Normally, an annual budget was set up for each work unit, and deviations from that budget were carefully examined and analyzed to determine what had happened and whether remedial action was required. The basic assumption was that what had happened in the past was a predictor of what was to happen in the future.

Long-range planning (which became popular around the 1950s), on the other hand, focused upon anticipating growth and beginning to manage the uncertainties and complexities found in most organizations. The basic assumption here was that historical trends would continue into the future. The planning process involved projecting sales and costs into the future based on data and experience from the past. The planning goal was then to develop actual plans that would address the expected growth or decline within the organization. The time frame normally used in long-range planning was more than the 1-year period for short-term planning and budgeting and control systems—typically 2, 5, or sometimes 10 years would be used depending on the organization and its circumstances.

Strategic planning (which surfaced in the 1960s) focuses on the identification and use of strategic thrusts and competencies within the organization in developing organizational plans. The underlying assumption here is that extrapolations made from past data and experiences alone are inadequate bases for future planning. As the external and internal environments change, there will be departures from past patterns, requiring strategic adjustments such as new or changed products, additional facilities, new markets, and so forth. Strategic planning, then, focuses on the entire environment of the organization, requiring knowledge of all the factors that have an impact upon the organization. Setting up internal operations as discussed in Chapter 1 is one of the best remedies for effective strategic planning, which emphasizes continued recognition of current internal operations and present business conditions, but adds to it the ability to anticipate the need for strategic changes.

Strategic planning, like long- and short-term planning and budgeting and control systems, while subject to continual review and ongoing adjustments, is also normally conducted on a periodic basis, usually annually. A liability of the periodic planning process is that the need for strategic planning and related decision making does not always fall neatly within the predesignated planning period. Accordingly, the strategic planning process must be flexible to cope with ongoing strategic threats, opportunities, and surprises. In effect, the planning system must work closer to *real time* so that it can effectively deal with changes in the organization's external and internal environments. What is needed is strategic flexibility so that the organization can respond quickly to sudden changes. In addition, strategies also need to be proactive, allowing the organization to create change rather than just respond to it.

The development, evaluation, and implementation of strategic planning and related business strategies are the heart of successful and effective management. Strategic planning is the cornerstone of a management system that assists managers within the organization to

- develop vision for their organizations;
- understand the dynamic and changing environment in which they manage their organizations;
- consider and decide upon strategic alternatives that are responsive to the environmental conditions that affect the organization; and
- adopt strategies that are based upon competitive advantages and that will be sustainable.

To be fully successful in the use of strategic planning techniques, it is helpful to put aside the belief that strategic planning merely represents an automatic extension of what was done last year and is primarily a statement of financial objectives and updated mathematical budget spreadsheet calculations from the prior year. This kind of incremental thinking not only inhibits the strategic planning process, but also prevents organizational creativity and innovation from optimizing strategic change. In reality, the start of the strategic planning process will typically begin outside the organization in the identification of opportunities, constraints, trends, and other changes with the purpose of creating strategies that are responsive to the organization's ever-changing but currently perceived needs.

> **STRATEGIC PLANNING USES THE INTERNAL AND EXTERNAL ENVIRONMENTS FOR ORGANIZATIONAL GROWTH**

What Is an Organization Strategy?

An organization's strategy, which is often referred to as its competitive strategy, takes into account the following elements:

1. *Products or services*: The scope of the organization is defined by the products or services it offers and chooses not to offer, by the market (customer or client base) or population it seeks to serve or not to serve, by the competitors it chooses to challenge or avoid, and so forth.
2. *Strategic investment thrust*: Although there are many different investment options and variations that can be considered, the following represent the range of possibilities:

   - *Growth or expansion*: Investing to enlarge or enter a new market
   - *Stability*: Investing only to maintain the existing position in the market
   - *Retrenchment or harvest*: Minimizing or reducing investment to deplete or downsize the organization
   - *Divestiture or liquidation*: Curtailing investment by recovering as much of the asset base as possible by closing down or selling off the business

3. Functional competence: Specific methodologies upon which to compete may be based on one or more functional area strategies such as:

   - Product line or services offered
   - Market positioning
   - Pricing
   - Distribution or logistics
   - Manufacturing or service delivery
   - Technological competence
   - Quality or reliability

4. Unique competitive advantage: A strategic skill is something that an organization does exceptionally well, such as manufacturing, service

delivery, quality control, or marketing and promotion, and which has strategic importance to that organization. A strategic asset is a resource, such as recognized name (brand name), or well-satisfied customer or client base, which creates an exceptional advantage over competitors.

THE STRATEGY DETERMINES THE PLAN

Strategies for Competitive Advantage

As you can imagine, there are many different strategies that an organization can adopt to achieve an advantage over competition. However, many types of strategies share similar characteristics that drive the strategy and provide the competitive advantage. Among these differing strategies to be considered, many would fall into the following two categories:

Differentiation Strategy

Differentiation strategy is when the product or service to be provided is differentiated from the competition by various factors which increase the value to the customer or client, such as enhanced performance, quality, prestige, features, service, reliability, or convenience. Differentiation strategy is often, but not always, associated with higher price. The desire is to make price a less critical factor to the customer.

Low-Cost Strategy

Low-cost strategy achieves a sustainable cost advantage in some important element of the product or service. Low-cost leadership position can be attained through high volume (high market share, perhaps), favorable access to lower cost raw materials or labor markets, or state-of-the-art manufacturing procedures. Low-cost strategy need not always be associated with charging lower prices, as lower product or service costs could also result in increases in profits, marketing, advertising or promotion, or product development investment.

Although most planning strategies usually involve differentiation or low-cost strategy, there are many other kinds of strategy that could be exploited. Examples include specific organizational competencies such as creativity and innovation, global perspectives, entrepreneurial spirit, research capability, sophisticated systems, automation and IT computer systems, and so forth. Within this framework the following three strategies which are not easily categorized as either differentiation or low-cost strategies could be considered in formulating strategic long-range plans.

Focus

This strategy involves organizations that focus on either a relatively small customer base or a restricted part of their product or service line. For example, a retailer selling to tall men or small women, or a CPA offering personal financial planning services to highly compensated individuals would be employing a focus strategy. The particular focus is usually the driving force in the planning effort, though differentiation or low cost may also be part of the strategy.

Preemption

A preemptive strategic move is the first implementation of a strategy into a business or service area that, because it was first, produces a distinct competitive advantage. Normally, for such a preemptive move to create an advantage, competitors should be inhibited or precluded from matching or countering the move. Some examples might be tying up the major distributors in a new market area before the competition can make a move, becoming the sole source for a particular product such as a new computer software package, or being the only professional firm in town that is a member of a professional practice management association (assuming such membership provides a distinct advantage). Being able to pull off such a preemptive move will put your competitors at a substantial disadvantage.

Synergy

The benefits of synergy (where the total is greater than the sum of its parts) can occur when an organization has an advantage due to its connection with another organizational entity within or outside the com-

Differentiation
Quality
brand name/reputation
customer orientation
installed customer base
patent protection
augmented protection
peripheral services
technical superiority
distribution
product line breadth

Low cost
No-frills product
product design
raw material source control
government subsidy
locations
product innovation/automation
own/control competitors
cost containment/low overhead
experience advantage
low cost culture

Competitive
strategic
advantage

Focus
Product focus-
market focus
geographic focus
customer focus

Preemption
Service
product
production
innovation
franchising
distribution
supply systems
customer loyalty

Synergy
Enhanced value
reduced cost
reduced investment
combined resources

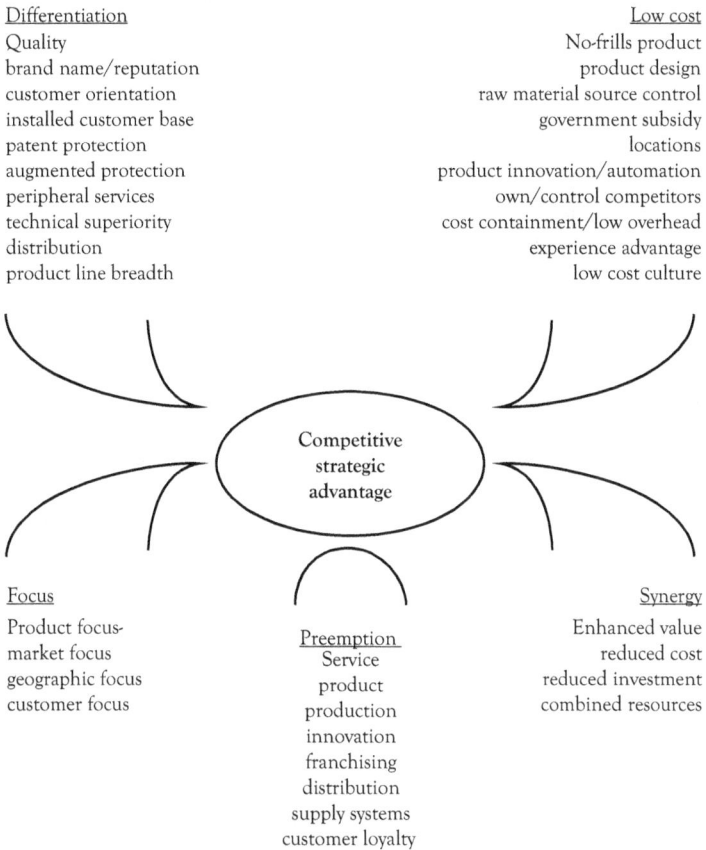

Figure 2.1 Strategies for competitive advantage

pany. The two entities may share sales and marketing efforts, research and development capabilities, office and support staff and facilities, warehousing, and so on. With the element of synergy, the two or more entities may be able to offer the potential customer the products or services that are desired, which neither might be able to do alone. For example, a more traditional retail electronics seller might link together with a computer software development firm to provide clients with full computer systems development services. The combination could create a synergy that would not exist if each worked separately. Figure 2.1 shows these strategies graphically.

In developing specific strategies for an organization, unique characteristics and trends relevant to the business must be identified. This normally requires some front-end analysis to be able to determine exactly what strategies would likely be most effective. Some factors to consider include the following:

- *Market orientation*: The organization's awareness of its external environment, including customers, competitors, and the marketplace. The goal here is to develop customer sensitive strategies that utilize the organization's market strengths.
- *Proactivity*: Attempting to influence events in the environment as opposed to merely reacting to forces as they occur. Examples would be lobbying for changes to a law that would significantly affect the organization, or trying to exploit a situation that at first glance appears to have totally negative implications (e.g., providing environmental cleanup, toxic waste disposal, or waste management services).
- *Information systems*: Identifying existing information systems and their ability to provide accurate and timely data for an effective strategic planning process. This includes determining what information is required, how to provide it, processing and analysis requirements, and so forth. Another factor to consider is the ability to provide online data so that strategic changes can be made more responsively.
- *Entrepreneurial style*: Entrepreneurial style emphasizes the organization's need to be more responsive to opportunities and not let unwieldy management systems bog down the decision-making process.
- *Multiple strategies*: Use of multiple strategies rather than a single strategy with related financial projections may help the development of the most effective overall strategy. The focus, however, should be on the strategy development and not on the financial projections.
- *Implementation capability*: While proper strategy development is extremely important, it provides no more than a theoretical set of alternatives unless they can be implemented. For the process to work, the strategy must first fit the organization's needs and opportunities and then must be capable of being implemented effectively.

> ### THE CORRECT STRATEGY
> ### WITH THE CORRECT IMPLEMENTATION
> ### CREATES THE CORRECT SOLUTION

Benefits of Strategic Planning

It is evident that effective strategic planning can be a long and arduous process for management staff that already has enough to do on a daily basis—as they may tell you. And it can become extremely frustrating in today's environment because of constant changes that make attractive future directions difficult to identify, let alone predict. The process itself requires communication, cooperation, and interaction among all the functions within the organization and can cause internal conflicts and resistance. Many times the alternative of simply waiting for and reacting to conditions as they occur seems more efficient, effective, and simple for producing results. What then are the benefits of implementing strategic planning?

1. Evaluation of strategic choices
2. Long-range vision
3. Effective resource allocation
4. Establishing an effective organizational communication system, both horizontally and vertically
5. Development of strategic management and related control systems
6. Enabling the organization to cope with change
7. Allowing proactive strategy development
8. Providing for online decision making
9. Identification of the needs for managing a complex organization
10. Enhanced strategic analysis and decision-making capability

The Strategic Planning Process

In addition to a discussion of the basics of strategic planning and some of the benefits that can accrue from its effective use, we should also deal with some of the mechanics of the strategic planning process. An overview of the strategic planning process is presented as follows that depicts the external and internal analyses (often referred to as a *situation audit*) that provide the inputs into strategy development, strategic decisions, and related strategic management.

External Analysis

External analysis involves a review of the relevant elements external to the organization, focusing on the identification of opportunities, threats, strategic questions, and alternatives. As much as there are many external factors that can be considered, it is important that the external analysis not be overdone, since this could result in substantial costs in terms of time and resources. Some elements that could be reviewed in an external analysis include the following:

> *Customer analysis* involves identifying the business's customer or client base and their needs. Particular emphasis should be placed upon products or services desired, quality and service considerations, special requirements, and so forth.
>
> *Competitive analysis* includes the identification of competitors, both existing and potential. Areas that could be included in competitive analysis are intensity of competition, competitors' performance, their objectives (i.e., are they the same as yours?) and strategies employed, strengths, weaknesses, and so forth.
>
> *Industry analysis* focuses on determining the potential of the industry in general and the products or services within the industry. For instance, will your organization and others be able to earn sufficient profits, or is the industry or product or service so competitive that attractive profits are unlikely to be attained? Elements that can be included in the analysis are industry size or potential, growth prospects, competitive intensity, barriers to entry (or to exit), threat of substitution, the power of suppliers and customers, cost structure, distribution or marketing channels, and industry or product or service trends, and key success factors (such as quality, service, customer relationships, etc.)
>
> *Environmental analysis* focuses on factors outside the organization that may create opportunities for or threats to it. This analysis must

necessarily be limited so that it doesn't become excessive in terms of time and scope. Areas that could be included are technological changes (impact of new developments), regulatory issues (effect of new or pending legislative initiatives), economic factors (effects of general economic conditions), cultural or social considerations (what's *in* or *hot* in the market), demographic trends (age patterns, socioeconomic changes, population pattern shifts, etc.), or geographic factors (rust or sun belt patterns, urban, suburban or rural changes, weather, transportation considerations, etc.)

Internal Analysis

Internal analysis involves achieving a detailed understanding of those areas of strategic importance within the organization. An examination of corporate strengths and weaknesses and their impact on the strategic issues is a relevant part of this process. The appropriate considerations can be categorized as follows:

Performance analysis which evaluates the performance of the organization in terms of financial results (e.g. return on investment) as well as other performance measures such as market share, product line analysis and performance, cost information, product development, management systems, personnel capability, and so forth.

Determination of strategic options which focuses on a review of those elements of the organization that influence strategy choices, such as past and current strategies; strategic problems which, if uncorrected, could cause significant damage (e.g., insufficient professional staff or other resources); organizational capabilities and constraints; financial resources and constraints; flexibility to change; strengths and weaknesses (build on strengths or neutralize weaknesses); and so forth.

**EXTERNAL AND INTERNAL ANALYSIS
PROVIDES THE CORRECT STRATEGY**

A graphic overview of these processes is shown in Figure 2.2.

EXTERNAL ANALYSIS
- customer analysis
- competitive analysis
- industry analysis
- environmental analysis
  - technological
  - regulatory
  - economic
  - cultural/social
  - socio-economic
  - geographic
- OPPORTUNITIES, THREATS
  & STRATEGIC QUESTIONS

INTERNAL ANALYSIS
- performance analysis
  - return on investment
  - market share
  - product line analysis
  - cost structure
  - systems
  - personnel capability
- determination of strategic
  options
  - past & current strategies
  - strategic problems
  - organizational capabilities
    & constraints
  - financial resources
- STRENGTHS, WEAKNESSES
  & STRATEGIC QUESTIONS

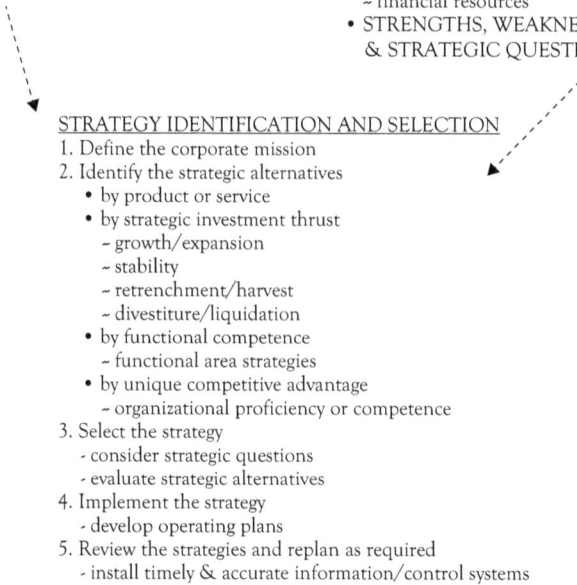

STRATEGY IDENTIFICATION AND SELECTION
1. Define the corporate mission
2. Identify the strategic alternatives
   - by product or service
   - by strategic investment thrust
     - growth/expansion
     - stability
     - retrenchment/harvest
     - divestiture/liquidation
   - by functional competence
     - functional area strategies
   - by unique competitive advantage
     - organizational proficiency or competence
3. Select the strategy
   - consider strategic questions
   - evaluate strategic alternatives
4. Implement the strategy
   - develop operating plans
5. Review the strategies and replan as required
   - install timely & accurate information/control systems

Figure 2.2 Overview of the strategic planning process

Strategy Identification and Selection

The five steps of an external and internal analysis are as follows:

1. Define the corporate mission

2. Identify the strategic alternatives

3. Select the strategy

4. Implement the strategy

5. Review the strategies and replan

Corporate Mission

The recommended first step in an effective external and internal analysis is to *define the corporate mission:* "Why are we in existence and what is our purpose?" A good mission statement usually defines the areas in which business is conducted, how the business is conducted, and what makes it unique. In addition, the mission statement can state growth directions, organizational philosophy, behavioral standards and ethics, human relations philosophies, financial goals, and so forth. The following is an example of an organizational mission statement—the Ritz-Carlton Credo:

> The Ritz-Carlton Hotel is a place where the genuine care and comfort of our guests is our highest mission. We pledge to provide the finest personal service and facilities for our guests who will always enjoy a warm, relaxed yet refined ambience. The Ritz-Carlton experience enlivens the senses, instills well-being, and fulfills even the unexpressed wishes and needs of our guests. We are ladies and gentlemen serving ladies and gentlemen.

MISSION STATEMENTS CAN BE INSPIRING BUT IMPRACTICAL

Management's efforts at motivational slogans are wasted if words cannot be turned into action

American management has spent countless man-hours and consulting dollars to create these inspirational slogans that they insist are mission statements. They emerge from the think tank armed with no more than a few simple declarations, hoping their articulation will confer flexibility in the organization and lend meaning to the everyday activities of the work force. Many so-called mission statements are ambitious visions of a utopian business state—nebulous, feel-good credos designed to inspire employees but lacking any actionable component. Others are sincere attempts to reestablish a sense of direction for companies seemingly rudderless. But the best of them, experts say, are clear, simple compelling statements of values and beliefs—and nothing more.

(Continued)

The mission statement should provide some direction and gives some sense of purpose and some feeling of a positive future state. The mission statement should cause you to ask, "How am I going to do that?" But it shouldn't *tell* you how to do that—that's up to the customers. As a kind of corporate mantra, mission statements have gained a lot of popularity in recent years as management searches for more clever ways to inspire, unify, and motivate employees. Their popularity signals a return to corporate roots, a reflection of management's realization that it may have strayed too far afield in expansionary times. The most common shortcoming of the corporate mission statement, experts say, is its lack of precision. Many mission statements fail in their attempt to articulate the basic principles intended to serve as guideposts to employees. They suffer from an overambitious attempt to be all things.

Strategic Alternatives

The second step, *identify the strategic alternatives*, could include the following considerations:

- Strategic investment thrust (i.e., growth or expansion, stability, retrenchment or harvest, or divestiture or liquidation)
- Competitive advantage strategies, such as in functional areas (sales, service, quality), or use of assets and skills, differentiation, low cost, focus, preemption, and synergy, each discussed previously

Select the Strategy

Some criteria to consider in the third step of the strategy identification and selection process, *select the strategy*, include the following:

- Responsiveness to opportunities and threats
- Use of competitive advantage
- Consistency with mission statement and objectives
- Feasibility and realism
- Compatibility with the internal organization
- Consistency with other company strategies

- Organizational flexibility
- Use of organizational synergy
- Exploitation of organizational strengths and competitor's weaknesses, and
- Minimization and neutralization of organizational weaknesses and competitor strengths

Implement the Strategy

Step four, *implement the strategy,* involves converting the selected strategies into operating plans. These operating plans consist of the organizational and departmental goals, objectives and detail plans that are necessary to move the organization toward meeting their strategic goals and objectives. To support these operating plans, resources must be allocated that are sufficient (but not excessive) to ensure successful working of the operating plans. This is the process of budgeting.

Review the Strategies and Replan

Finally, the fifth step of the process, *review the strategies and replan*, as required, involves development and implementation of an adequate and timely information system that allows management to measure progress toward strategic plans and related operating plan goals, objectives, detail plan activities, and budgets.

Tools for Internal Analysis

An integral part of organizational internal analysis is the assessment of the strength of each element of its product or service mix. This type of evaluation—*portfolio analysis*—attempts to examine the business in the following areas:

1. Evaluation of business position and market attractiveness.
2. Resource allocation—which organizational units should receive resources, which generate resources, and from which resources should be withheld.
3. Establishment of strategic recommendations based on strategic investment allocation decisions.

There are many methods in use to help managers carry out their strategic planning responsibilities. Two of the more established and recognized are the BCG (Boston Consulting Group) product portfolio matrix and the strengths, weaknesses, opportunities, and threats (SWOT or WOTS-up) analysis. While these tools provide help in evaluating strategic alternatives and providing general direction to managers, it must be clearly recognized that every organization is unique, and strategic development must be specifically fashioned to meet the needs of the particular organization at a specific time in its development. Tools and techniques provide assistance and direction—they do not provide prescriptive solutions to the organization's needs.

The BCG Product Portfolio Matrix

The BCG matrix model is easy to understand, uses appealing terminology, and can be easy to quantify if the organization has necessary market growth and market share information for its products and services. The model assumes that market growth and market share is a strong indicator of product or service strength. An example of a product portfolio matrix is shown in Figure 2.3. Note that the matrix is sectioned into four quarters and that the products are represented by different sized circles (with the size of the circle representing the relative sales volume). Each of the quadrants is identified with the following terminology:

a. *Question marks*: having a low share of a high growth market. These products typically generate negative cash flow because of their development needs and their relatively low volume, and their future success is not clear. The products in this segment are sometimes further subdivided into *problem children* (those with slim chances of long-term success) or *prize heifers* (those with strong success probabilities). These products represent the long-term future success of the company, and must therefore be carefully evaluated, screened, culled, and developed as deemed proper by corporate management.

b. *Stars*: having a high market share of a rapidly growing market. These are the bright lights in the company's portfolio of products. They get the press coverage, generate excitement among the stock market

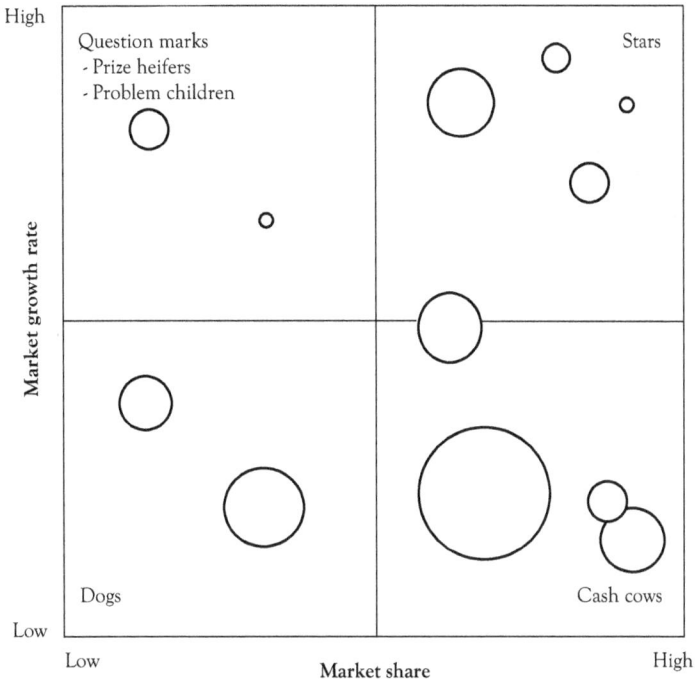

Figure 2.3 BCG product portfolio matrix

analysts, and add luster to the company's annual report. They are typically quite profitable, but do not generate significant positive cash flow because of their continuing development and promotion cash needs. Without a reasonable amount of stars in the overall portfolio, the company's immediate future is clouded.

c. *Cash cows*: having a large share of a low growth market. These products are the engine room of the company—strong, steady, dependable, but often dull, prosaic, and unexciting. They are mature, well known in the market place, generally fully developed, and generate substantial cash for the organization. They provide the cash fuel needed to fund the development of stars and prize heifers. Without a stable of cash cows, the company may be unable to adequately fund new product development.

d. *Dogs*: having a low share of a low growth market. These seem to be the losers in the mix, and often they are. However, they may be necessary to maintain product continuity or to keep a full range of products in place. They are likely to generate low or negative cash flow and must be carefully managed to avoid a destructive impact on the company's overall cash position or market image. If they generate some positive cash flow and enhance the overall portfolio in some other way, they may be worth keeping. Or it may be possible to regenerate interest in the product with an infusion of development or marketing effort. Otherwise, a graceful demise should be planned.

Once the products or services have been categorized, the next step is to analyze the strategic implications. In general, the primary strategy is to utilize the cash from the cash cows and fund the prize heifers and the new stars. The prize heifers should be managed into stars, and problem children should be turned into potential stars or abandoned. The stars must be managed to become the company's future cash cows, and the current cash cows should be milked and fed so that their largesse will continue as long as possible. The dogs need to be reinvigorated if feasible—if not, plans for their elimination must be put in place.

The BCG product portfolio matrix model provides schematic assistance for the organization's management of cash and the identification of strategies for product or service investment and disposition. It can help to determine which products are cash users and which are cash providers (and why); and it can help the organization intelligently determine how available resources should be deployed among products to maximize long-range future success.

> **MILK THE COWS,**
> **REACH FOR THE STARS,**
> **LET THE DOGS OUT**

Exercise

Examine the product portfolio mix depicted in the BCG product portfolio matrix exhibit and determine what kinds of strategic alternatives you might suggest for the company. What are its strategic strengths and what weaknesses can you see based on the information provided? Where do you think the company should concentrate its strategic efforts?

Suggested Response

This company very likely is experiencing excellent financial results—good profitability and good cash flow—because of the significant impact of cash cow products. Anyone reviewing the financial reports, including company management, is likely to be happy with the results and complacent about the future of the company because of its financial success.

However, the product portfolio matrix analysis shows a different set of prospects for the company. The relatively small amount—in number and volume—of stars is disturbing with regard to the immediate future of the company since there is not a lot of follow-up strength to the present cash cows (which will eventually move into the dog category). Additionally, the long-range prospects of the company may be even more at risk. The number of products is distressingly low and should be of great concern to company management. With only two products in this category, if even one is a problem child, risk notches up significantly.

While it is necessary to have more information about the specifics of the company and its products (nature of the products, their prospective life cycles, their growth prospects, their profitability, etc.), it appears that significant effort needs to go into new product development to build up the stars and *question marks*. This improvement in long-term new product prospects is essential to the company's long-term viability.

The dog category needs to be reviewed to determine if these products continue to add value to the company. If so, they can be maintained. As long as they are not creating a drain on company resources, they do not represent an issue of immediate concern. But if they are draining cash or other resources, they need to be phased out or reinvigorated back to star or cash cow status.

An interesting and significant aspect of the product portfolio matrix approach is that it shows information that is not discernible from the company's financial statements. Financial statements show historical, not prospective, information. That is one reason that a financial analysis of the company is itself not enough to present a comprehensive picture of what is going on. While clever and extensive financial analysis can be useful in determining possible future scenarios, the future remains unknown to us all. But the product portfolio matrix gives a much more reliable look at company prospects as they relate to sales and products than does a financial review.

SWOT or WOTS-Up Analysis

This analytical process is an acronym for strengths, weaknesses, opportunities, and threats. SWOT analysis assists the organization in determining what are the environmental conditions, internally and externally, that must be dealt with and also how best to deal with them. The more competent the organization compared to its competitors, the greater the chances for success.

The *internal* environmental conditions and considerations can be classified as follows:

a. *Strengths*: which are resources or capabilities the organization can take advantage of to achieve strategies, goals, and objectives.
b. *Weaknesses*: which are limitations, faults, or defects within the organization that may prevent it from achieving its strategies, goals, or objectives.

The *external* environmental conditions and considerations, normally beyond the control of the organization, can be classified as follows:

a. *Opportunities*: which are favorable conditions in the organization's external environment. These may be trends or changes of some kind, or overlooked needs that justify the demand for a product or service and allow the organization to enhance its position.
b. *Threats*: which are unfavorable conditions within the organization's external environment that are potentially damaging to its strategy or its position in the market.

Effective use of SWOT analysis involves identification of as many as possible of the company's strengths, weaknesses, opportunities, and threats and then finding a strength that can be exploited to take advantage of an identified opportunity. This is a classic example of niche strategy. A strength can also be used to create a demand in the market if conditions

	Internal	External
Positive	**Strengths** - strong sales/marketing - brand name recognition - customer preference - high quality image - strong post-sales service - abundance of cash	**Opportunities** - economic upswing - increased consumer income - international interest - positive health benefits identified - principal competitor has class action suit filed
Negative	**Weaknesses** - large inventories - excess capacity/personnel - resistance to change - heavy reliance on single product line - relatively high sales price - unproductive research	**Threats** - increased domestic competition - technological advancements - market saturation - aging population - takeover interest - growing overseas sales and manufacturing capability

Figure 2.4 Exercise: SWOT or WOTS-up analysis

permit (i.e., consumers are truly interested). On the other side of the analysis, the company can take steps to eliminate or reduce internal weaknesses, and should make a strong effort to mitigate, avoid, or somehow cancel identified threats. An example of a SWOT analysis is shown in Figure 2.4.

While this example is an admittedly limited SWOT analysis—a more realistic situation would generate much longer lists in each quadrant—it is interesting to speculate on possible strategies. For example, if the company were to embark on a new product development campaign, it could be viewed as follows:

- *Strengths*: Each of the company strengths would be beneficial to new products developed and marketed; and the abundance of cash could be the source of funds to pay for the development activities.
- *Weaknesses*: With the possible exception of large inventories, each of the weaknesses could be addressed and overcome, at least in part, by a successful and innovative new product development program.
- *Opportunities*: A well-designed new product program could take advantage of each of the items listed in the opportunities

column, including taking advantage of a competitor's mis-
fortune—if that is consistent with the company's ethical
standards.

- *Threats*: Most of the threats could be addressed as well. For
example, aging population could be turned into an opportunity by developing a product for that segment of the
population. In addition, any takeover interest by others is
(temporarily) to be mitigated by using up the abundance of
cash on product development, though success in the program
could ultimately increase takeover interest even further. But
that is a future problem to be addressed by another SWOT
analysis.

In summary, an effective product development program can address
possibly 80 or 90 percent of the factors listed in this SWOT analysis.
This is an unrealistically high *hit ratio* in practical terms. But the idea of
developing a strategy or strategies based on a SWOT analysis is almost
certain to lead to broader and more effective results than trying to develop
answers to specific individual concerns. That is the beauty of a SWOT
analysis, along with its simplicity and the fact that it works—even in the
absence of significant amounts of quantitative marketing data.

WOTS-UP DOC
SEIZE THE OPPORTUNITY

Review of the Elements of Strategy Development

There are many elements that can be researched and analyzed in the
development of the organization's strategic plans. However, one can take
this approach too far and never get to the development of the actual strategic plan. However, there are some areas that should be included in your
review of factors related to your strategic planning, such as:

a. Customer analysis
1. What are the major market segments?
2. What are customers' motivations and unmet needs?

  b. Competitor analysis
  1. Who are existing and potential competitors?
  2. What strategic groups can be identified?
  3. What are their levels of sales, growth, market share, and profits?
  4. What are their strengths, weaknesses, and strategies?

  c. Market analysis
  1. How attractive is the industry and its submarkets?
  2. What are the structures, entry and exit barriers, growth prospects, and profitability potential?
  3. What are the alternative distribution channels and their relative strengths and weaknesses?
  4. What industry trends are significant to strategy?
  5. What are the current and future key success factors?

  d. Internal analysis
  1. What are our present performance levels?
  2. What has been our strategy?
  3. What are our assets and skills?
  4. What are our weaknesses?
  5. What are the characteristics of our organization such as structure, personnel, culture, values, and systems?
  6. What is our cost structure?
  7. Does a cost advantage exist or can one be developed?
  8. What are our strategic problems, constraints, and questions?
  9. What are our strengths and weaknesses relative to our competition?

  e. Environmental (external) analysis
  1. What environmental threats, opportunities, and trends exist?
  2. What major environmental scenarios can be conceived?
  3. What are the major strategic questions and information need areas?

  f. Strategy development
  1. What alternative growth directions should be considered?
  2. What should be our business mission?
  3. What investment level is most appropriate—growth or expansion, stability, retrenchment or harvest, or divestiture or liquidation?

4. What competitive advantages should be developed?

5. What skills or assets need to be developed or maintained?

6. What are the key strategic questions?

7. What strategies best fit our strengths, goals and objectives, and our organizational style and culture?

ANALYZE, ANALYZE, ANALYZE,
PLAN, PLAN, PLAN,
AND THEN EXECUTE

Situational Analysis: Planning Questions

In analyzing the present situation of the subject organization, the following are some suggested questions that could be used to assist in gathering data as to the specific situation that the company finds itself in.

a. Industry

1. Does the organization have a clear idea of the market in which it is operating?

2. What is happening to the industry in which the organization is operating? Is it growing or declining? What are the expectations about it? Compared with last year?

3. What is the current size of the market and the organization's market share? Has the organization acquired a greater market share over the past years or has its share declined? Compared with last year, what changes have there been in the organization's market share? Has market share declined or grown compared with last year?

4. Compared with last year, has the competitive position changed?

5. How much of an idea does the organization have of the impact of political and economic trends upon their prospects?

6. What are the chances of legislative controls changing during the planning period?

7. How good an idea does the organization have of the likely changes in the social environment over the planning period?

8. Does the nature of the product sold in the industry vary from year to year?

9. How do you rate the ability of the company to define likely future sales?

10. Over the past years how closely have the organization's products followed the price trends in the market?

11. What degree of seasonality is apparent in the industry?

12. How extreme are the long-term fluctuations in the demand for the particular product or service?

13. How much money is the company spending on research and development in relation to competition?

b. Market

1. How clear an idea does the organization have of the functional divisions in the market and the type of product or service that it demands?

2. When was the last time that the organization sought customers' views on its products?

3. What are the effects on the profitability of the business in lowering and raising price on volume of sales?

4. Is the organization knowledgeable of the effects of lowering price on volume?

5. How does the quality of the organization's products or services compare with competitive products or services selling at more or less the same price?

6. How much of the organization's product range is sold at a significant discount (i.e., 25 percent off list price)?

7. How closely has the organization analyzed the potential profitability of a change in credit policy?

8. How closely has the organization analyzed inventory levels to achieve the level of service that it considers necessary in the market place?

9. Has the organization considered potential financial and marketing benefits in its product distribution methods?

10. Does the organization know the costs of current delivery methods and of individual deliveries?

11. Have alternative distribution methods been considered?

12. How much of overall sales are provided by products more than 10 years old? Five years old? Three years old?

13. What is the level of control over new product development?

14. To what extent are brand opportunities exploited?

15. To what extent do major customers (5 to 10) contribute to the organization's sales and profitability?

16. What amount of sales are achieved from outside the organization's immediate geographic area?

17. What system exists for evaluating the effectiveness of the sales effort?

18. What are the specific service standards established for employees?

19. What system exists for monitoring operational performance?

20. Has the organization considered the potential for improving the speed of service by technological innovation?

c. Production

1. What percentage of production is accurately estimated in terms of direct costs like material, labor, machine time, and so forth?

2. What proportion of the total cost of production of the normal production run is made up of startup or setup costs?

3. To what extent is the capacity of the existing plant or machinery fully utilized?

4. Are the amounts of raw materials and components effectively evaluated as to minimums required to maintain production?

5. Does the organization evaluate the range of products it produces in relation to the effects on production efficiency?

6. How much of the finished goods inventory is over six months old?

7. What system of quality control is used over products and services?

8. Does the organization evaluate in-house manufacture versus outside purchase opportunities?

9. How many suppliers does the organization depend on for the bulk of its raw materials and components?

10. How much of the organization's products and services are produced in the most efficient method?

11. How much has labor productivity increased over the last year?

12. By how much would replacing the current machinery improve efficiency?

13. To what extent could production efficiency be improved by better physical layout or a change in facilities?

14. Does the organization consider using outside help to improve production processes?

d. Financial analysis
   1. How easy is it to manage and understand the accounting system?
   2. How accurately is cash flow analyzed and controlled?
   3. How have overheads, expressed as a percentage of sales, changed over the last three years?
   4. What measures are used to assess the various elements of operational performance?
   5. What is the change in the level of bad debts over the last three years?
   6. What system is used to evaluate capital investment opportunities and how are decisions made?
   7. Is the tax and pension planning structured to maximize the return to the organization?
   8. Does the organization have a stated policy relative to additional financing and borrowing?

e. Personnel
   1. To what extent are employees involved in the planning process?
   2. To what extent do employees feel involved in what the organization is doing?
   3. Is there a form of profit sharing among the employees?
   4. To what extent is the nature of each individual job defined and the authority and responsibility that go with it?
   5. How does the organization review personnel requirements for the future?
   6. How many (number or percent) have done exactly the same job for over 10 years? 5 years? 3 years?
   7. What are the organization's recruitment procedures?
   8. How many employees have received no training over the last year? Two years? Three years?
   9. What is the level of absenteeism for illness over the past few years? Level of accidents?
   10. What are the employee grievance procedures?
   11. How well does the organization understand its legal obligations relative to personnel concerns?

**I KNOW THE QUESTIONS,
NOW I NEED SOME ANSWERS**

Potential Areas for Competitive Advantage

The following areas could be considered individually or together while identifying areas for competitive advantage.

1. Reputation for quality
2. Customer service or product support
3. Name recognition or high market profile
4. Good management
5. Low cost production capability
6. Strong financial resources
7. Customer orientation
8. Breadth of product line
9. Technical superiority
10. Solid base of satisfied customers
11. Segmentation focus
12. Product characteristics
13. Continuing product innovation
14. Market share
15. Distribution systems
16. Low cost and high value
17. Understanding or knowledge of the business
18. Pioneer in the industry
19. Operations adaptable to customer needs
20. Effective sales force
21. Flexibility and entrepreneurial culture
22. Marketing skills
23. Strong market image
24. Engineering or research and development capability
25. Good human relations—staff and customers

**TO THINE OWN SELF BE TRUE,
BUT KNOW THY COMPETITORS**

Characteristics of a Customer-Driven Organization

As previously mentioned, one of the major reasons for the organization to be in business is customer service. To follow up on this principle, the company may want to become a customer driven organization. If so, here is a checklist of various areas to consider.

a. **Understanding the customer**
   1. Maintain contact with the customer.
   2. Know product or service attributes that are important to the customer.
   3. Understand important elements of customer choice.
   4. Understand different segments of customer business and adjusts strategies accordingly.
   5. Listen to customer and work on solving problems.
   6. Identify and address unmet customer needs.

b. **Knowing the customers' perceptions of your company**
   1. Know how the organization is perceived by customers and clients.
   2. Know why the organization is perceived as it is.

c. **Delivering quality or value**
   1. Does the organization truly care about what the customer receives in quality and value?
   2. Do quality and value measure the impact on goal and objective setting within the planning system?
   3. Is Customer satisfaction measured regularly?
   4. Is the organization responsive to customer input and feedback; are customer suggestions and complaints included in organizational strategic planning?

Conclusion

Strategic (long-range) planning usually encompasses a future period of three to five years or more, although the actual period will vary according to the particular business. Traditionally, upper management handles the strategic planning process, though other operating personnel as well as outside assistance can be used to improve the resultant quality of the plan. In long-range planning, all aspects of the business's activities are addressed, including areas such as

- organizational expansion or contraction;
- products or services to be provided, including additions, changes, and deletions;
- markets in which to conduct business;
- capital investments and expenditures;
- facility requirements;
- research and development activities;
- personnel and employee relations and benefits;
- return on investment;
- sales, expenses, and profits;
- financing needs.

Long-range planning is a complex undertaking because of the unpredictability of the future. The farther out the planning period from the present, the greater the risk of uncertainty. Because of this uncertainty, and because even ordinary conditions change over time, long-range plans must be periodically reviewed and adjusted by management.

Management also needs to take other risk factors into account in planning the future, such as

- economic conditions: inflation, growth or recession, unemployment, interest rates, national budget deficit, trade deficits, value of the dollar, and so forth;
- changing market conditions;
- technological advancements and developments;
- political factors: legislative changes, tax changes, regulation or deregulation, environmental action, minimum wage, employee benefit concerns, antitrust activity, and so forth.

The company's long-range planners will have to collect, analyze, and interpret all available information to be used in forecasting the future. Sources include internal historical data and reports related to sales and costs, product line analyses, financial data, personnel data, information regarding production and delivery of goods and services, and so forth. In addition, the planners may use more sophisticated mathematical forecasting models and other analytical techniques such as break-even analyses, return on investment calculations, and ratio, change, and trend analyses to provide data for the decision-making process.

As an output of the strategic planning process, top management should develop broad goals for the long-term operations of the organization, and these goals should be communicated to all lower levels of management and other operations personnel as appropriate. Long-term goals address areas such as

1. desired size and scope of operations;
2. customer relations;
3. personnel and employee relations;
4. products or services to be offered: existing, new, eliminations, changes, new product development, or product enhancements;
5. quality control considerations;
6. capital investment plans;
7. customer base: existing, new, changes, eliminations;
8. research and development activities;
9. marketing or sales efforts;
10. capital structure and sources of financing.

By providing long-term direction, top management establishes an effective framework within which operations management and staff can make informed and intelligent decisions relative to developing their own divisional or departmental plans and budgets. Top management should also request operating personnel to identify present problems and causes together with related recommendations for corrections, and should get the latest updated information regarding changes and trends, sales and costs, production or delivery conditions, personnel needs, and so forth.

If effective communications systems have not been established between top management and the remainder of the company, the strategic planning process may result in long-term goals that do not fully relate to the organization's needs. Also, operating personnel may then have to work with goals that they disagree with and believe will not work. This can prove to be disastrous in today's competitive marketplace where businesses of all sizes need to become more effective planners if they hope to grow and prosper—or simply survive.

This chapter has provided a discussion of the long-term strategic planning processes—leading toward the short-term plan and its corresponding budgets. In the succeeding chapters, we will explore each of these elements in greater detail so that you will be able to implement the procedures into your own organization.

> **INTERNAL OPERATIONS BEGETS STRATEGIC PLANNING WHICH**
> **BEGETS SHORT-TERM PLANNING WHICH**
> **BEGETS DETAIL PLANS AND BUDGETS**

An overview of the organizational planning cycle is shown in Figure 2.5.

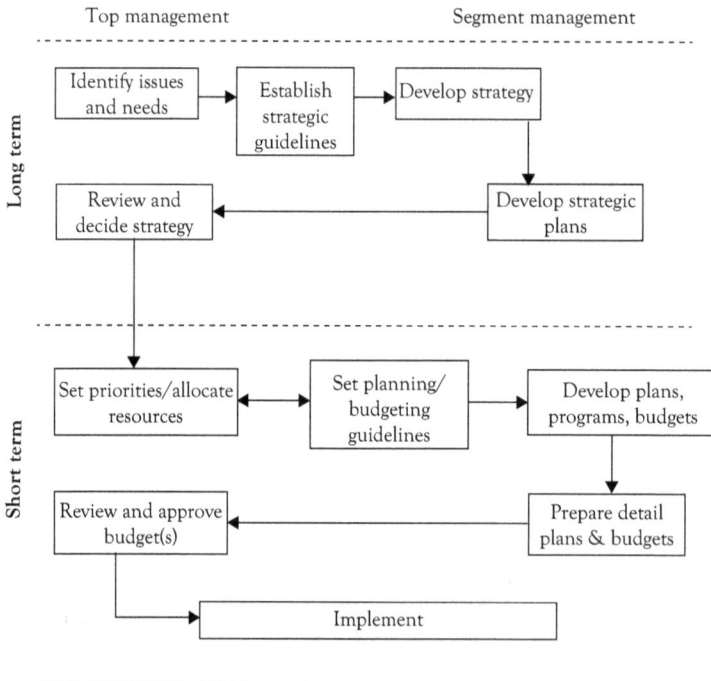

Figure 2.5 Organizational planning cycle

CHAPTER 3

The Short-Term Operating Plan

The purpose of this chapter is to examine some of the shorter term activities (a year or less) that are necessary to support the overall planning process for the organization. Planning without implementation is an academic exercise that will result in little, if any, benefit to the company—other than some nice papers for the files. Breaking the plan into short term and detail phases is necessary if implementation is to take place, and it is this aspect of the planning process that will be discussed in this chapter.

The objectives of this chapter are to

1. examine the underlying theories behind short-term planning;
2. review the elements of a short-term operating plan and some of the factors to consider prior to implementation;
3. identify the factors to consider before beginning short-term planning;
4. identify benefits of and potential problems in a short-term planning process;
5. describe the major steps of a short-term planning system;
6. discuss the implementation of a short-term plan.

**THE SHORT TERM PLAN
IS THE FIRST STEP
IN ACHIEVING THE LONG-TERM PLAN**

Introduction

The long-range goals and strategies established by top management need to be translated into more specific short-term departmental goals and objectives. Definitions of goals and objectives are presented subsequently. Note that goals are broad directions or outcomes that the organization wishes to attain, while objectives are measurable and time-specific results relating to one or more of the desired goals. Normally, short-term goals and objectives are developed for a specific planning period (often annually) for both the entity as a whole and each departmental unit. But keep in mind that as they are plans, such plans are subject to change and must be monitored on a continual basis. Just as top management has responsibility for developing the long-term goals (with input from operating personnel), so do operating managers and staff have the responsibility for developing and implementing the short-term goals and objectives within the framework of the overall long-term plans

Goals and Objectives

Goals

- Statements of broad direction
- Describing future states or outcomes of the organization to be attained or retained
- Indicating ends toward which the organization's effort is to be directed

Objectives

- Measurable, desired accomplishments related to one or more goals
- Whose attainment is desired within a specified time frame and can be evaluated under specifiable conditions

Characteristics of Objectives

- *Measurable*: Attainment (or lack thereof) can be clearly identified
- *Explicit*: Clear indication of who, what, when, and how
- *Time-Specific*: To be accomplished within a stipulated period of time

- *Realistic*: Capable of being attained within the time frame specified and with the expenditure of a reasonable and cost-effective amount of effort and resources

To demonstrate the relationship between long-term and short-term goals and objectives, let's look at an example. A long-term goal of the company may be *to become the industry sales leader in our consumer product line.* A related medium-term goal might be *to increase on a steady basis the sales, in units, of our consumer products.* A specific short-term objective for this planning cycle then could be *to increase sales units of Sheen facial soap by at least 10 percent over last year.*

This last objective can be the basis for specific detail plans and related performance expectations for the sales department, finance, manufacturing, and other affected functions within the organization. Departmental objectives can be converted into levels of production, inventory quantities, labor needs, manufacturing capacity, sales activity, administrative support, and other short-term needs. These short-term objectives and related detail plans then become the starting point for the budgeting process. The budget will reflect what is necessary (in terms of labor, material, overhead, engineering, sales, administrative, and other costs) to meet the agreed-upon short-term objectives and work the detail plan for successful results. When management approves each budget, it will reflect the authorized level of expenditures needed to fulfill the objectives by following through on agreed upon detail plans. At this point each manager and supervisor presumably will have been delegated the authority to incur the expenditures to make the detail plan work. Finally, the managers and supervisors can be evaluated based on their ability to effectively work their plans to achieve established short-term objectives.

THE DETAIL PLAN
MOVES TOWARD THE OBJECTIVE,
THE OBJECTIVE MOVES TOWARD THE GOAL

A schematic of the planning cycle is shown next (Figure 3.1). This schematic graphically depicts the relationship between strategic planning and the short-term planning process. It also shows the interactive

Top management | Combined | Segment management

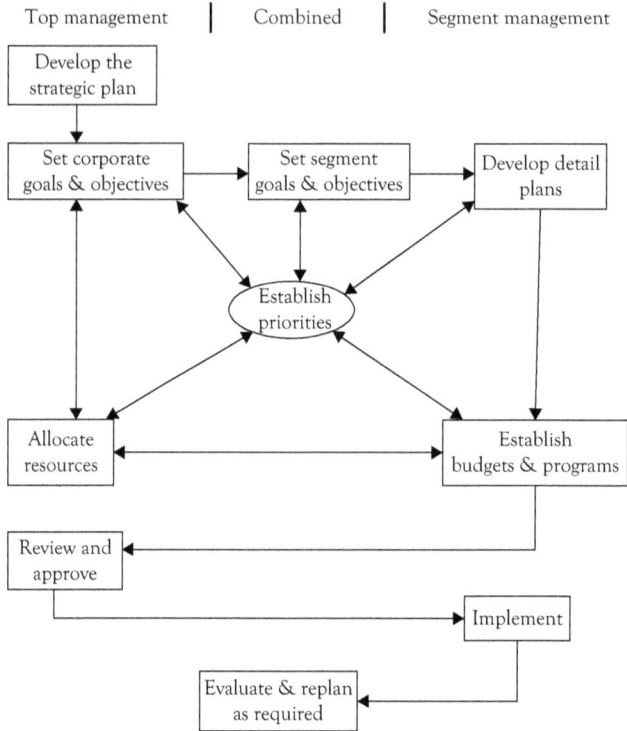

Figure 3.1 Short-term planning cycle

relationship between top and segment management that is required to make the entire planning process fully effective.

The Organization Planning System

One of the most important benefits of an organizational planning system is that it forces managers, supervisors, and operating personnel in the organization to take the time to consider strategic questions and alternatives for achieving the most effective results. Without this focus, day-to-day operations (and related crises) would normally consume all the available time. An organizational planning system enables management to respond to both the external and internal environments, and allows managers to run a complex organization with the aim of achieving an integrated and coordinated result—despite ceaseless changes, nerve-wracking uncertainty, and all-too limited resources.

Organizational planning is the term used to describe planning for the organization as a whole, and encompasses decision making at all levels of the organization. Within this framework, strategic planning provides the basic direction and focus of the organization—that is, the big picture! Strategic planning is concerned with top management decisions relative to the future direction of the organization in terms of such things as business focus, resources, products and services, and markets. Long-range planning, which is often thought of as synonymous with strategic planning, more typically provides a time frame for the strategic plan, typically three to five years (but possibly much longer, depending on the nature of the business).

Short-term planning, or operational planning, provides the framework for implementing the strategic and long-term plans into a short-term time frame—usually a one-year operating period. It should be a direct derivation from the strategic plan and is the logical next step in converting top management's strategic decisions into short-term operating actions. The operating plan works with present resources and the current situation to create a detailed blueprint for achieving agreed-upon goals and objectives for the various segments of the organization. It is the effective development of the short-term operating plan that we will discuss next.

The budgeting process involves activities such as revenue projections, expense allocations, determination of the need for other sources of funds, and the projection of profit or loss, financial position, and cash flow for the organization. Budgeting will be discussed in greater detail in the following chapter. Note, however, that budgeting alone is not planning! While budgeting is a critical activity for the organization, it is only one element of the short-term operating plan. There are many organizations, however, both large and small, that continue to confuse budgeting with planning, or they may allow the budget to be done first and thus have the budget dictate the planning process rather than reverse the sequence and properly have the budget emanate from the planning process.

Presumably, as the organization grows in size and complexity, management will realize that crisis management and purely intuitive planning and control are no longer sufficient. More structured planning concepts and techniques might find their rightful place in the organization's recurring business development activities.

**SOUND INTERNAL OPERATIONS,
STRATEGIC LONG-RANGE PLANS,
SHORT-TERM OPERATING PLANS,
HOW TO DETAIL PLANS, AND
BUDGETING = THE PLANNING CYCLE**

The Underlying Theory Behind Short-term Planning

The starting point for the short-term planning cycle is the strategic or long-range plan as developed by top management. The next step is to develop corporate and segment goals and objectives that support the strategic plans. These are normally formulated by top management with built-in feedback to allow lower levels of management to review the goals and objectives and assure that they are consistent with operational needs—and that no constraints exist that could prevent successful attainment. Once these plans are in place, priorities must be established so that senior and segment management know the extent of resources that need to be allocated to allow the goals, objectives, and detail plans to be attained.

The short-term planning system at the segment level is a process in which lower levels of management develop detail plans in accordance with their own understanding of what top management requires of them. Senior management then exercises top-down direction to support the broad framework of total organizational objectives. In this two-way flow of ideas, a deeper understanding is achieved as to the nature of the organization and how each organizational unit plays a supportive role in accomplishing what the organization wants to achieve.

Segment mission determines segment purpose and functions, and from these plans, budgets and programs are derived. This in turn leads to implementation, review, and replanning. The combination of bottom-up development and top-down direction and review is the foundation for the effectiveness of short-term planning procedures. It maximizes involvement of managers, supervisors, and operational personnel in developing operating goals, objectives, and detail plans; while, at the same time ensuring that these are compatible with overall organization mission and strategic plans, as well as shorter term goals and objectives.

Effective short-term planning necessitates participative management. This does not necessarily mean a complete change in the management system, but it does place more emphasis on certain management techniques such as getting things done through other people. Managers must delegate in order to derive the greatest benefit from the planning system. They must give their employees freedom to devise their own methods for attaining their goals and objectives. This carries with it, of course, the freedom to fail—frightening to some, but a major learning process for employees.

THE GREATER EMPLOYEE INVOLVEMENT,
THE GREATER THE RESULTS

The Short-term Operating Plan

Short-term planning is the process whereby top management, operating management, and personnel in the organization jointly identify common goals and objectives, define each individual's major areas of responsibility in terms of results expected, and use these measures as guides to operating each organizational unit and assessing the contribution of each staff member. Short-term planning also permits management at all levels of the organization to concentrate on those matters requiring attention and to devote only minimal effort to those activities that are running smoothly. This concept is popularly known as management by exception. Note that the process is based on a cooperative relationship between top and functional management, insuring an integrated plan for all levels of the organization. As a result, all members of the organization are working toward the same targets—that is singing out of the same songbook.

The general steps normally required in the short-term planning process are discussed in detail as follows:

> *Planning*: Based on corporate goals and objectives, each segment will state its mission (its reason for existence) and its major functions; will analyze its strengths, weaknesses, opportunities and threats; and will develop its goals and objectives (specific goals to be attained).
>
> *Programming*: Once management agrees on the segment goals and objectives, segment staff will develop alternatives as to how they will accomplish their objectives. Through a priority-setting process,

they should consider existing constraints (obstacles to success) and prepare cost-benefit analyses to determine the optimum detail plan or set of activities that will accomplish the objectives.

Budgeting: After the detail plans have been agreed to, resources need to be allocated to each activity. During the budget process, revenues are projected, priorities are set (how much can we do with limited resources?), resources are allocated to relevant activities (expense budgeting), and additional sources of funding are identified if required. Established budgets should represent the delegation of authority from top management to segment management to carry out their agreed-upon plans. This integrates the planning and budgeting phases of the entire process.

Implementation: Following agreement and approval of the detail plans and related budgets, the segment becomes responsible for implementing the plan. Since the steps and activities of the detail plan have been agreed to as the optimum way for the organization to achieve desired objectives, segment personnel must be held accountable for making the plans work as effectively as possible.

Evaluation: The evaluation process in a short-term planning cycle consists of establishing effective reporting systems that will inform if objectives are, in fact, being met. Based on these evaluations, management can determine if the plan should be continued, changed, or dropped entirely. This is the replanning process, which is the start of a new planning cycle.

Factors to Consider Before Short-term Panning Begins

Short-term planning is not an easy process to put into effect in an organization. There are several factors that should be taken into consideration before proceeding with the installation of this system of management planning.

1. *Sustained top level management support*: Ultimate responsibility for the successful implementation of short-term planning systems cannot be delegated to lower levels within the organization. The process should be undertaken *only* if the individual(s) at the top are fully committed to devote sufficient time and resources to ensure its success.

2. *Patience*: Normally only modest results are achieved in the first year other than to get managers and staff thinking and acting in terms of goals, objectives, and detail plans, and to provide time for the planning concepts to become engrained. Improved results should accrue during the second year. Outstanding results should be realized by the third year if the short-term planning process has been properly developed and supported.

3. *Management control*: Those responsible for achieving plan results must have substantial control over the factors affecting achievement of goals, objectives, and detail plans (including related budgets) for which they are to be held accountable.

4. *New management style*: Effective use of short-term planning methodology requires a change in management style from traditional production-oriented methods to a result-oriented goals approach. This is perhaps the most important requirement for effective use of short-term planning methods. At the same time, it is also the most difficult for managers to implement. Some of the more significant changes that must be made to the traditional management approach are as follows:

   • Managers and others at multiple levels need to participate in the development of goals, objectives, and detail plans for their departments, work units, or both.

   • Managers should be given freedom within broad guidelines to devise their own methods for achieving goals and objectives.

   • A major role of managers should be to teach and counsel their employees; just as they also may need teaching and counseling by top management.

TOP MANAGEMENT SUPPORT AND PARTICIPATION RESULTS IN OPERATIONAL PARTICIPATION

What Short-term Planning Can Provide

Considering all the problems and changes required to implement an effective, result-oriented planning system within the business, what then are the benefits that can be identified to justify the time and expense required for successful installation?

1. *Effective planning*: Short-term planning provides for realistic goals and objectives and outlines detail plans for the improvement of activities at all levels of the organization in a way that integrates all the planning pieces.
2. *Communication*: When the manager and operating personnel reach a clear understanding among themselves and top management on the functions and objectives of the organizational units, they avoid the kind of misunderstanding that too often occurs when there is no real agreement on what constitutes a job well done.
3. *Involvement*: The short-term planning system encourages management, supervisory, and staff people to participate in establishing goals, objectives, and detail plans as well as doing the implementation work.
4. *Delegation*: Managing within a short-term planning system makes delegation easier and safer. When a manager gets agreement about functions to be performed, objectives, and ways to measure their achievement, the work can be delegated without fearing loss of control.
5. *Objective evaluations*: In traditional management systems, people are often evaluated in terms of their personal characteristics, and many times there is little equity or objectivity in these evaluations. An effective short-term planning system, on the other hand, allows recognition of and reward for measurable results.
6. *Other benefits*.
   a. Organization
   - Improvement in managerial effectiveness
   - Focused managerial effort
   - Increased profit potential
   - Coordinated effort by team members
   - Objective reward criteria
   - Establishment of responsibility and accountability
   - Identification of individual advancement potential
   - Awareness of individual development needs

b. Segment managers
- Motivation for them and their staff members
- Clearly defined areas of accountability
- Establishment of clear areas of responsibility
- Strengthened relationships—upward and downward
- Effective coaching framework
- Elimination of personality-based evaluation systems

c. Operating staff
- Expanded knowledge and expectations
- Provision of specific performance measures
- Clarification of responsibility and authority
- Increased possibility of job satisfaction
- Identification of specific reward and achievement factors

**EFFECTIVE SHORT-TERM PLANNING
PRODUCES LONG TERM RESULTS**

Reasons Why Short-term Planning May Fail

As we have previously stated, the short-term planning process requires many factors to be in place within the organization in order to be successfully implemented. Before proceeding with the implementation of a short-term planning process, some of the reasons why short-term planning programs fail should be identified in order to help prevent recurrence of the same problems.

1. *Goals, objectives, and detail plans set by directive:* In those cases where top management is manipulative or directive in setting segment goals, objectives, or detail plans, real commitment to organizational goals and objectives is rarely achieved. Staff personnel become distrustful and cynical and tend to treat the planning system as an imposed burden, rather than a performance-oriented target. Improvement in performance, if it happens at all, is usually short lived.

2. *"Soft" objective setting:* If management fails to provide overall guidance and fails to adequately review and critique objectives, resultant

segment objectives may not be sufficiently challenging. The objectives then do not contribute to the achievement of optimal results.

3. *Failure to control results*: Some planning systems generate impressive reports, but do not provide for effective control and follow-up action to create performance improvement. Other planning systems provide for control by individual employees, but management may fail to respond to operating personnel control reports with appropriate reactions, suggestions, or both. The planning process then gradually withers and disappears.

4. *Unrewarded performance*: An effective short-term planning system is result-oriented and requires full management commitment to organizational objectives. Staff personnel can become quickly disenchanted if they do not see a direct correlation between achievement of objectives and reward decisions.

5. *Packaged short-term planning approaches*: The short-term planning system must be tailored to the needs of the specific organization. Although a standardized approach can identify criteria to consider and methods to use, an individualized final package is invariably required.

6. *Inflexibility of short-term planning systems*: External and internal environmental conditions change as do organizational responsibilities, authorities, and reporting relationships. The short-term planning system must be sufficiently flexible to adapt to such changes, or it will become irrelevant, unrealistic, unproductive, and, ultimately, unused.

7. *Hurried implementation*: Because of the extensive training time and experience required for the short-term planning process to become fully effective, implementation must be phased in at a rate suitable to available resources and requirements. The first step should be effective goal and objective setting with related formulation of detail plans. Training and implementation, measurement, control, and appraisal should be spread over the first one to two years. Too rapid a pace for implementation often results in delayed realization of planning benefits, with the resulting discouragement often the cause of a complete breakdown in the process.

8. *Insufficient management commitment and involvement*: Where support from the top of the organization is superficial, short-term planning

systems inevitably fail to achieve the desired results. Commitment to planning means much more than approval—it means putting planning activities at the top of the corporate "to do" list. Probability of failure without full commitment by management is so high that formalized short-term planning should not be considered without it.

> ## WITHOUT EFFECTIVE PLANNING PROCEDURES, THERE WILL NOT BE EFFECTIVE RESULTS

Implementing the Short-term Planning System

There are four major steps in implementing short-term planning systems at the segment level in the organization, namely

  a. stating mission and functions;
  b. developing segment goals and objectives;
  c. converting objectives into detail operating plans;
  d. measuring progress toward achievement of objectives.

Stating the Mission and Functions

Short-term planning implementation begins with a statement of mission and functions for each operating unit of the organization. The mission can be defined as a statement of purpose and responsibility of the segment. The functions are all the major responsibilities of the units that are required to carry out the mission. Many times this becomes one of the most beneficial exercises in the total planning process, as it requires each manager and staff member to analyze the role of the unit in relation to the overall mission of the organization.

Developing Segment Goals and Objectives

The next step is the development of goals and objectives, which is usually done one year at a time and which involves either improvement to an existing situation or correction of an activity that is below acceptable standards. Objectives are specific in that they focus very closely on the actual effort required to carry out the responsibilities of the segment.

Development of objectives (and related detail plans) should go hand in hand with the development of the budget. Hence, the resources allocated to the segment must support every objective. If a change in the resource allocation is required to support the achievement of objectives, allocation revisions must be approved concurrently with the approval of the objectives.

Regular goals and objectives are those that relate to the segment's routine functions. They should not be in conflict with regular duties and responsibilities; rather, they should be an integral part of these activities. After these regular goals and objectives have been defined, it may be desirable to establish one or more special objectives for the period. Special objectives generally involve one-time projects of particular importance to the organization. Therefore, they should be limited in number. Development of a new reporting system is an example of a special objective. Wherever possible, objectives should be quantified so that performance can be measured. For example, four objectives may be needed for a particular department:

- Reduce the number of person-days lost from 150 to 75.
- Increase the number of actual production hours available from 50 to 55;
- Control operating expenses: Do not exceed $180,000 compared with the existing level of $200,000.
- Implement a quality control system that will enable rejected customer deliveries to be less that 1 percent of total shipments.

Establishing explicit objectives in terms of dollars, hours, or pieces will generate greater likelihood of achievement than will generalized statements of desired objectives, expressed in percentages or nonquantitative terms. With such careful quantification of objectives, it is easier to follow progress toward achievement throughout the planning and implementation period.

After establishing objectives, recognize that they may have different degrees of importance within the organization, so it may be necessary to determine their relative values. This should be a joint process between the staff member and the manager. One possible approach is to assign a point value to each objective as illustrated in the following. In the example, the first objective is given a weight of 10—that is, the importance of that objective is considered to be 10 percent of all objectives in that organizational unit. The total of all the weights for the objectives in any unit must add up to 100.

Example: Weighing of objectives

Goal: Optimize the IT computer facilities.

Objective	Point value
1. Reduce man-days lost	10
2. Increase processing hours available	5
3. Control operating expenses	20
4. Institute quality control system	5
5. Improve staff capability	10
6. Upgrade equipment	15
7. Install security system	5
8. Establish off-site back-up facility	15
9. Set up periodic review procedures to ensure we stay up-to-date	5
10. Create management information Steering Committee	10
Total	100

Objectives to encourage higher performance and to force corrective action should receive relatively high weights. Nominal weights are given to significant but lower priority activities where average performance is acceptable or to areas not requiring special attention at this time.

WEIGHING OBJECTIVES DOES NOT FATTEN RESULTS

Nonquantifiable Objectives

Some objectives are, by their nature, not quantifiable. An objective calling for the development of a quality control system is an example. Progress toward the achievement of such an objective can be followed by monitoring a schedule of events. If, for example, the development of a reporting system is subdivided into five steps, completion of each step could constitute 20 percent of the target.

For example:

Objective: Develop a quality control system by 12/1/xx.

Step	Event	Target
1	Establish requirements and specifications by 3/1/xx	20%
2	Investigate other control systems by 5/15/xx	40%
3	Design system by 9/1/xx	60%
4	Test system by 11/1/xx	80%
5	Obtain approvals from eng., mfg., and sales by 11/15/xx	100%

By definition, achievement of a nonquantifiable objective is limited to 100 percent, which on the surface eliminates the possibility of overachievement. However, a completed objective can also be eligible for a quality rating if the work contribution toward the achievement is considered outstanding enough to merit it.

A NONQUANTIFIABLE OBJECTIVE
CAN STILL BE ACHIEVED

Converting Objectives Into Detail Operating Plans

Development of objectives will not produce significant results unless the objectives are turned into a detail operating plan and implemented. In setting up a detail plan, the department manager and staff must determine what general approach should be taken to attain the objectives. They usually deal with ways to raise performance, improve quality or scope of services, or reduce operating costs. An example of an operating plan is depicted below for one objective.

Example: Operating plan details

Objective: To reduce days lost from an average per employee of eight per year to five per year for the fiscal year beginning 7/1/xx

Operating plan details:

	Completion deadline
1. Research absenteeism history	1–31
2. Research attendance incentive systems	2/28
3. Develop an appropriate attendance incentive system	3/30
4. Obtain management approval for the proposed system	4/30
5. Develop orientation program for employees	5/30
6. Conduct orientation program	6/5–6/15
7. Implement system	7/01
8. Provide follow-up program	from 7/01
9. Monitor and control absenteeism	from 7/01
10. Provide counseling services for abusers	from 7/01

The first step is to identify events that must be completed to achieve the objective. An estimate of time requirements for completing each event follows and deadlines are established for each event. The same process is repeated in establishing detail operating plans for each objective. Normally a number of alternative detail plans are developed, (usually two or three), so that department management and top management can arrive at the best priorities and allocation of resources.

Measuring Progress Toward Achievement of Objectives

The final step, after implementing the detail plans, in setting up the short-term planning system is to develop an effective follow-up system. Continual evaluation of progress toward achievement of objectives is essential for effective use of a short-term planning system. Since managerial evaluation should be based on achievements in relation to agreed-upon goals, objectives, and detail plans, periodic performance evaluation is crucial.

Progress reports should be prepared periodically, but not less than once a month. These reports should indicate to what extent agreed-upon objectives have been attained to that time.

In very large and complex organizations where the kinds of functional activities of each unit vary across a wide spectrum, it is virtually impossible to apply a single rule to every situation. Rather, the judgment and discretion of the reviewing personnel need to be fully exercised in dealing with extreme cases of over-and underachievement. The important point that the unit manager and staff need to understand is that top management requires a balanced effort on their part in relation to all important elements and functions of their units. An erratic pattern of performance often reflects the manager's personal likes and dislikes, but does not adequately serve the purposes of the unit.

One of the major benefits of a systematic follow-up program for the short-term planning system is that it creates the vehicle for necessary dialogue between the employee, segment management, and top management. In this context, management can most effectively play its role in motivating staff and exploring ways of removing obstacles to higher achievement. Also, in these review procedures, objectives can be reexamined to test whether they are realistic and feasible in light of any changed conditions. If the short-term planning system is to remain valuable, the segment manager and staff should be prepared to revise detail plans and objectives. The implementation of an effective monitoring system that allows changes to be made can avoid fostering the fatalistic attitude that departments must live out the rest of the year repeatedly explaining variances that have resulted from inappropriate detail plans and related budgets or changes in environmental conditions.

> ## WITHOUT PROGRESS AND EVALUATION, AN OBJECTIVE IS JUST AN OBJECTIVE

Departmental Situational Analysis

The purpose of a departmental situational analysis is to determine the department's capability to achieve a high level of performance in its key results areas. In the situational analysis, the advantages, or those factors that may enhance positive performance, are identified as strengths or opportunities, and the disadvantages, or those factors that will impede performance, are identified as weaknesses and threats. Such an analysis is known as Strengths, Weaknesses, Opportunities, Threats SWOT analysis.

Such an analysis should be completed for each key result area. The following data show the results of an analysis for the manufacturing department relative to manufacturing costs:

Strengths	Weaknesses	Opportunities	Threats
High volume	Labor turnover	Sales potential	Lack of money
OK work force	Material shortages	Product name	Unstable economy
OK mfg. space	Poor layout	New equipment	Strikes
Good standards	Limited tooling	Better training	Changing labor
OK supervision	No capital budget	Plant layout	Obsolete design

Properly done, such an analysis assists the department in the correct identification of the areas to consider in developing specific objectives. They also provide guidelines as to what level of achievement each objective should be given. In addition, the analysis should help to prioritize those areas that are the most critical and, therefore, should be considered first. For example, the aforementioned analysis discloses two major weaknesses of labor turnover and material shortages. These should be considered as immediate areas to remediate.

SWOT ANALYSIS
HELPS SWAT THE BUGS

Guidelines for Setting Objectives

Here are some guidelines to use in setting objectives.

1. Be sure that objectives in one business segment or work unit are not in conflict with objectives in another area of the organization or with the organization's overall goals.
2. Avoid too many objectives; exclude marginal or less relevant ones.
3. Concentrate on the objectives that meet essential needs.
4. Avoid destructive competition. Each business segment should be competing only with itself against performance standards. If too much stress is placed on segments or individuals attaining their objectives to the exclusion of all else, significant amounts of goodwill, cooperation, and morale may be lost.
5. Include some objectives that direct and encourage joint effort and cooperation so that employees are rewarded for working together. Otherwise cooperative employees may no longer find the time to

help others, since they may be too busy pursuing their own goals, objectives, and plans.

AVOID INTERNAL COMPETITION
OR IT WILL KILL THE PLAN

Questions Regarding Preparation of Objectives

In developing good short-term planning objectives, you can evaluate the formulation of your objectives by asking the following questions. If no is the answer to any of the questions, the reason why should be analyzed and the objectives revised.

a. Is the objective stated in terms of specific end results to be accomplished?
b. Is the objective clear enough to suggest certain types of action? Is the objective a guide to action?
c. Is the objective ambitious enough to represent a challenge?
d. Is the objective stated so that progress can be measured?
e. Is the objective realistic, practical, and focused on important results?
f. Does the objective has economic value?
g. Is the objective related to one or more organizational and segment goals and the organization's strategic plan?

IS THE OBJECTIVE OBJECTIVE?

Key Operating Indicators Results Areas

One of the most important steps in developing objectives is the identification of key operating indicators (KOI) and results areas, which are those highly selective areas of a department's operations where a strong level of performance must be achieved to optimize results. The most valuable purpose these KOIs serve is to help work unit personnel direct their limited resources to the most important matters where the return will be the greatest relative to the efforts expended. In this way, they help prevent personnel from falling into the activity or "busy-ness" trap—getting busy and staying busy without first determining what to be busy about.

It is normally easier to identify and select KOIs using a two-step approach:

1. List major job responsibilities or job functions, and
2. Examine each job function to determine the KOI areas.

This process is demonstrated next for a financial manager:

Major functions	Key results areas
Accounting	Accurate, timely measurement, and reporting of performance
Treasury	Cost of capital, availability of capital, and return on investable funds
Credit/collections	Aging of accounts and bad debt level
Information technology	Machine utilization, personnel utilization, and cost/benefit level

KOI results areas normally fall into the following categories:

Quantity: Revenue and production levels
Quality: Customer satisfaction and product quality
Timeliness: Schedule misses (or hits) and customer demands
Cost: Cost of services and manufacturing costs

**KEY OPERATING INDICATORS
ARE KEY TO OPERATIONAL RESULTS**

Examples of Measurement Techniques

I. Profit contribution and cost reduction
  a. Production and quantity
    1. Processing time
    2. Machine and employee downtime
    3. Actual versus optimal staff size
    4. Productivity (output per unit of input)

  b. Production and quality
    1. Error rates and rejects
    2. Losses (dollars, lost sales, etc.) resulting from errors

      3. Number of occurrences of errors

      4. Adherence to quality assurance procedures

  c. Costs

      1. Adherence to budget (on flexible budgeting basis)

      2. Overtime costs

      3. Materials and supplies costs

      4. Labor costs

      5. Overhead (manufacturing, selling, and administrative) costs

II. Accounting controls

  1. Adherence to audit schedules

  2. Number of exceptions

  3. Response time to correct exceptions

  4. Timeliness and accuracy of reports

III. Management controls

  1. Systems and methods improvements

  2. Personnel turnover rate

  3. Absentee rate

  4. Individual task performance

  5. Training programs

  6. Management and staff development

  7. Coaching and mentoring

IV. Coordination

  1. Understanding of operations

  2. Problems solved

  3. Sales forecast versus production schedule

  4. Customer relations, employee relations, and bank relations

  5. Inquiry delays

  6. Number of praises or complaints

Example: Statement of Mission, Functions, Goals, and Objectives: Accounting Department

Mission

To record all financial transactions of the company and maintain accurate financial records; to collect amounts and accounts receivable when due; to disburse funds for authorized purchases and services received; to provide timely financial reports and information for operational and financial planning, control and evaluation; to safeguard the assets of the company; and protect the company against foreseeable and unforeseeable losses.

Functions

1. Collections: To collect receivables promptly so as to keep the amount due to a minimum.
2. Payroll and payroll taxes: To calculate weekly, semimonthly, and monthly payrolls and to pay the wages and salaries when due; to prepare and file monthly, quarterly, and annual state and federal payroll tax returns, and to make payments when due.
3. Accounts payable: To record and pay all properly authorized vouchers for goods and services purchased and received.
4. Accounting records: To maintain accounting records and systems for accumulating data needed for financial statements, payment of bills, collection of receivables, filing tax returns, computing costs, and so forth.
5. Financial reports: To prepare and supply to management accurate and timely financial statements.
6. Financial analysis and planning: To analyze and interpret financial data, make recommendations for cost reductions, and control of operations.
7. Budgets: To advise and assist department and program management in the preparation of budgets based on approved short-term plans, to assemble and review budgets with appropriate company personnel, and to compile them into an overall budget as supported by the company's short-term plans.

Goals

1. To constantly improve the financial reports and financial data needed for the proper planning, direction, and control of the organization's operations.
2. To provide more accurate budget and actual cost data based on current activity levels and relationship to short-term plans, kept

constantly up-to-date, and integrated into a simple and effective management system.

Objectives

1. *Payroll and payroll taxes*: To maintain the present high standards of accuracy, timeliness, and reliability; to select and train a payroll clerk by October 15, 19x1.
2. *Accounts payable*: To review and analyze the accounts payable function so as to streamline operations and take advantage of computerized procedures by November 30, 19x1; to pay 95 percent of all bills due by the vendor's stated due date and to take advantage of all discounts during the 19x2 fiscal year.
3. *Accounting reports and systems*: To develop a simplified chart of accounts which will provide meaningful data for effective management control and will lend itself to computerization—completed by July 31, 19x1.
4. *Financial reports*: To establish and meet by July 1, 19x1, a fifth working day deadline for publishing financial reports and to maintain such a schedule for the balance of the fiscal year.
5. *Financial analysis and planning*: To set up formats for reporting to company management to take advantage of their recommendations for management planning and evaluation by June 30, 19x1.

Example of a Structured Set of Organization Goals

I. Corporate goals and objectives

G-1: To increase return on sales.

Objective: To increase the return on sales by 10 percent, for this fiscal year over last fiscal year.

G-2: To increase return on investment.

Objective: To increase the return on investment by 6 percent for this fiscal year over last fiscal year.

G-3: To provide positive organizational atmosphere so that each employee may grow and develop to the fullest of his or her ability.

Objective: To develop a comprehensive staff development program by 3/15

II. Segment goals and objectives
   A. Production department
   G-1: To increase productivity
   Objective: To increase the number of units produced of Item A per direct labor hour from four to six by January 15.
   G-2: To meet production schedules.
   Objective: To be no more than two days late on any production schedule during the   periods from December 1 through June 30, and to do so within budgeted costs.
   G-3: To improve quality control.
   Objective: To reduce rejected production items from 8 percent to 5 percent during the period from November 1 to February 1
   G-4: To increase production quality control.
   Objective: To reduce present level of rejected items in production from 8 percent to 3 percent during the period from November 1 through April 30.
   B. Finance Department
   G-1: To improve cost variance reporting.
   Objective: To report all cost variances within two days of the end of the reporting period beginning November 30.
   G-2: To increase return on investments.
   Objective: To increase return on invested cash from 10 percent to 12 percent during the next fiscal year by more aggressive investment activities and better cash management.
   G-3: To minimize tax costs.
   Objective: To reduce the present effective tax rate from 22 percent of profit before taxes to 18 percent in the next fiscal year.
   C. Marketing and Sales Department
   G-1: To increase market share.
   Objective: To increase market share of product line A from 24 percent to 28 percent during the period from November 1 to June 30.
   G-2: To increase total net sales dollars.
   Objective: To increase total sales dollars by 14 percent this fiscal year over last fiscal year, while at least maintaining the gross profit margin.
   G-3: To decrease advertising and promotion costs.

Objective: To decrease advertising and promotion costs from 5 percent of net sales to no more than 4 percent by March 31, and to maintain that level of costs for the remainder of the fiscal year.

Sample of a Detail Operating Plan:
Sales Department—Order Service Unit

Goal(s) Related to

2. To ensure that price quotations are issued as expeditiously as time and accuracy will allow and that the field sales force is informed daily of quoted deliveries within their districts.

Objective to be Achieved

4. Systematize the procedure for immediate Request for Quotation (RFQ) notification to the field sales force by August 15. This information will be used by sales people to contact customers. The success of the program is dependent upon field sales making effective use of the data provided.

Present Conditions

a. The customer service group work load, at times, becomes heavier and the requirement for RFQ information is not met.
b. Field sales people do not make a routine practice of requesting this information.
c. Manager, order service has no formal way to monitor the program to ensure that it is being carried out properly.

Desired Conditions

Order service receives quote requests by mail, phone, and fax. The requirement is to inform the field sales force on the day of receipt of RFQs, within the following categories:

a. New customers—all inquiries
b. Repeat customers
   i. RFQs for nonstandard parts
   ii. RFQs for standard parts, valued at $5,000 or more

With RFQ information furnished by order service, the field sales force is to contact the customer for further information.

Detail Operating Plan

1. To establish a formalized information method for RFQs and to implement a log system for this activity.
2. Assign this activity to the administrative staff to be handled on a routine daily basis from information supplied by the customer service group.

Activities	Dates	Budget
a. Design log format	7/5–7/8	$ 600
b. Brief administrative staff on their part of program	7/11	$450
c. Instruct customer service group to pass copies of all RFQs to order service administrator	7/11	$300
d. Implement procedures • Order service administrator: To divide quote requests into territories and pass to the secretary for logging • Set up an open territorial file for RFQs at the administrative desk • Instruct field sales force to contact the administrative desk as routine part of their call-in procedure • Scan log prior to 4 p.m. daily: To determine which sales people have not been advised of quote requests, and inform them by phone, • Send copies of completed logs to the sales manager for follow-up	7/11–7/29	$4,500
Total budget		$ 5,850

Measurement Techniques

To be measured by

a. initially meeting target date of August 1 for complete and successful implementation of the system;
b. periodically scanning logs monthly to determine same day notification or delayed notification. Expectation is for same day notification in all cases—any exceptions to be justified as to cause.

Constraints

  a. Success of program is dependent upon field sales force making the best use of the data provided.
  b. Time available within order service department to meet daily RFQ turnaround requirement.
  c. Ability to make contact with sales personnel on a daily basis.

Alternative Plans and Evaluation

  a. Have copy of RFQ routed to sales manager for notification to sales force. Considered impractical from control and logistical standpoint.
  b. Place burden on sales personnel to call in for quotes from representative order service personnel assigned to that territory. Considered unworkable due to unavailability of sales personnel calling in when order service personnel are available.

Sample of Detail Operating Plan Budget: Recruit an Accounting Manager

Responsibility: Joe Burns

Description: To recruit for one accounting manager at the annual accountants convention so that at least three highly qualified screened candidates are available for a final interview.

Standards:

  a. Candidates are evaluated at least "very good" by screeners.
  b. Candidates are available for final interview by August 20.
  c. Total cost for recruitment does not exceed $4,000.

Program steps	Responsibility	Dates	Budget
1. Prepare advertisement	TRC	7/10–7/16	$420
2. Place advertisement	TRC	7/20	$680
3. Write and print invitation	TRC	7/12–7/24	$380
4. Post invitation at convention	RSS	8/04	$870
5. Deliver invitation to assigned room	RSS	8/4–8/6	$220
6. Staff hospitality suite	RSS	8/4–8/6	$875
7. Confirm interview dates	RSS	8/6–8/8	$120
8. Send confirmed list to screeners	RSS	8/9	$40
Total			$3,605

Some Pitfalls of a Planning System

Top-Down versus Bottom-Up Systems

In a top-down system, top management creates strategy as well as departmental goals and objectives that they consider necessary to achieve their strategies. Although this procedure provides the resources to achieve the strategies across the organization, it is seen many times by department managers, supervisors, and staff as management by directive. Since the operating personnel have no input into the planning process, the resulting plans are seen as top management's, and there is little motivation for the operating people to achieve success—in fact, there may even be a subtle (or not-so-subtle) sabotaging of efforts. In a bottom-up system, the planning process starts at the lowest levels at which the organization operates. The theory is that operating people are closer, more responsive, and more knowledgeable about the immediate needs and are thus in a better position to develop plans. Since they are totally involved in the planning process, they will be more committed and motivated to make the plans succeed. The potential flaw here, however, is that top management commitment is also necessary to make the plans work.

Spreadsheet Driven Process

With the advent of the microcomputer and spreadsheet software, the planning process has become, for many organizations, a spreadsheet proliferation of income statements and balance sheets for years into the future. Focus tends to be more on projecting past financial data into the future than planning for the future. Elegant accounting methods, complex spreadsheets, and reams of data that are easy to generate, but nearly impossible to analyze and understand, take the place of considering and evaluating alternatives and making intelligent estimates of what is likely to really happen.

Financial Objectives Orientation

In many instances, organizations will set their goals and objectives relative to short-term financial measures such as sales, profits, return on investment measures, market share, and so forth. With these factors dominating, other goals and objectives often become vaguely stated or relatively insignificant in the planning process. Frequently, however, this zeal to improve short-term financial performance can be detrimental to production, marketing, product development, and other functions vital to the long-range future success of the enterprise.

Planning Rigidity

Organizational plans that are too rigidly followed may result in inhibiting actions that are necessary for the organization. What results is a defensive mindset on the part of many managers that manifests itself in an "it's not in the budget" attitude that tends to eliminate or sharply reduce proposals for change.

Lack of Commitment

Often an organization is very adept at producing excellent plans, but falls short in the implementation process. The result is an elegant set of plans sitting on the shelf unused. There may also be lack of commitment to making the plans work at the top or throughout the organization. The plans are not sufficiently integrated with detail operating plans, and there is not an effective control and monitoring system to make it successful. Another situation that may occur is that top management is not willing to enforce the process with requisite discipline. Whatever the cause, the result is a lot of wasted resources expended with no benefit to the organization

Conclusion

Preplanning by making your internal operations the most economical, efficient, and effective as possible using best practices in a program of continuous improvements as part of becoming a learning organization is the best starting point for effective planning procedures—starting with setting your planning parameters by long-range strategic planning. Based on this framework, management and operations personnel establish their short-term operating plans consisting of organizational, departmental, and functional goals, objectives, and detail plans—determined by all levels of management and operations working together to develop agreed upon short-term operating plans. The output of the short-term operating plan process is a set of agreed upon goals, objectives, and detail plans (the how to step) ready for implementation. The only ingredient missing is the budgeting of your detail plans based upon an allocation of scarce resources on a priority basis as to monetary and time commitment. The budgeting phase of the planning cycle will be discussed next.

SHORT-TERM PLANNING
REQUIRES LONG-TERM THINKING

CHAPTER 4

Budgeting and Profit Planning

The purpose of this chapter is to examine the budgeting process as an integral part of the overall organizational planning activity. The budget should be an outgrowth of corporate planning and should be fully integrated with the plan. A look at the budgetary process from a quantitative, as well as a philosophical point of view is included.

Some of the objectives to be accomplished are to

1. define budgeting in terms of how it fits into the planning activity;
2. explore the intricacies of the budgeting process;
3. examine the planning and control aspects of budgeting;
4. look at some of the advantages and pitfalls of budgeting;
5. review the budgeting process within an organization;
6. identify the use of budgeting for profit planning and cost containment;
7. discuss other budgeting applications.

**BUDGETING ALLOCATES
SCARCE RESOURCES TO THE PLAN**

Introduction

As previously mentioned, the short-term planning process is the beginning point for the budget process. As plans are developed for the organization, the budget (or financial plan) is developed as an immediate outgrowth. The types of budgets that may need to be developed include

1. the sales or revenue budgets that identify what products or services planned to be sold, in what quantities, at what price, and to whom.

It is the sales budget that determines the level of funds that will be generated to cover operating expenses. Obviously, if revenues exceed expenses, an operating profit will be generated; but, if the opposite is the case, the operating deficit will have to be covered from nonoperating sources, that is, borrowing, equity, or sale of assets;

2. the production budgets (if a manufacturing entity) that define the level of production or services to be provided, and take into account changes in the planned inventory levels;

3. the operating budgets that are used to determine the costs that must be incurred to meet the production requirements. They include the costs necessary to produce the goods or services—direct materials, labor, and overhead—either on a departmental or product line basis;

4. the selling, general, and administrative budgets that include marketing and administrative support expenses such as marketing or sales, accounting, personnel, legal, management information systems, executive, and so forth. Items included in these budgets are salaries, fringe benefits, supplies, travel, stationery, insurance, and so forth;

5. the capital budget that deals with the funds to be spent on capital requirements such as increased building capacity, new production or office equipment, computer processing equipment, new product lines, and so forth. Capital expenditures are those cash requirements for plant or equipment that will be used for a number of years in the future and will provide benefits for the company over those future years. Normally capital budget items have relatively high costs and are justified by time-factored discounted cash flow methods based on the lifetime benefits to the organization;

6. the research and development (R&D) budget that is typically developed as part of the strategic plan with expenditures planned to support and enhance development of new products and other business activities to help the company achieve its long-term objectives;

7. other project budgets that should be used for new products or services development, internal systems improvements, new manufacturing methodologies, promotional or advertising campaigns, or similar activities requiring the expenditure of significant amounts of money beyond the normal operating activity levels of the business;

8. the cash budget that provides the opportunity to examine the financial feasibility of the overall plan. Without sufficient cash to implement the plans, the company cannot survive. The cash budget allows management to see if sufficient funds are available and, if not, a plan to acquire the funds or adjust the plan;

9. the projected financial statements that pull the elements of the plan together and allow management to examine the profitability and financial position that will ensue if the plan is successfully implemented. This concluding look gives management a final opportunity to make changes or build contingencies into the plan.

**THE BUDGET IS MORE THAN
LINE ITEMS ON A PIECE OF PAPER**

Budgeting Overview

In a business organization, functional disciplines (sales, manufacturing, marketing, purchasing, data processing, accounting, etc.) are all interdependent. Therefore, all of these functions must work together to successfully achieve organizational goals and objectives. The overall plans of the organization must be clearly communicated so that management in each functional area is aware of what needs to be done to ensure smooth integration with other areas and for the entire organization. Effective profit planning and budgeting are among the tools used to coordinate the organizational plans and the detailed activities of each of the disciplines.

Budgeting Defined

The budget is a detailed plan depicting the manner in which monetary resources will be acquired and used over a period of time. The budget should be a quantitative manifestation of the next year of the company's strategic plan. It is part of the short-term operating plan. The *master budget* summarizes the organization's plans (goals and objectives) for the future time period—providing for the allocation of financial resources for agreed upon short-term operating plans. It is a statement of management's expectations and establishes specific targets relative to such things as sales, operating costs, production levels, general and administrative expenses, and other monetary transactions for the time period covered. Budgeting should result in projected financial statements—income statement, balance sheet, and statement of cash flow. In effect, the master budget reflects management's short-term plans for the operating period—and how these plans are to be carried out—expressed in financial terms.

Planning and Control

To be fully effective, the budgeting system must provide management with tools for both planning and control. At the beginning of the budget cycle, the budget is the plan or standard to be met based on the development of organizational short-term goals and objectives and the detailed steps to achieve these objectives. During the budget cycle, the budget is used as a control device for management to measure results against the planned objectives so that corrective action can be taken as required. At the end of the budget cycle, the final results are measured against the plan to determine if the goals and objectives were met, and, if not, why. The result of this analysis helps to establish a new and better budget for the next operating cycle. Good planning without proper control produces poor results; and budgeting without proper planning provides no legitimate objectives against which to measure progress.

Advantages of Budgeting

Managers of organizations that tend to operate in a crisis atmosphere or seat-of-the-pants mode, may believe that the budget process is a waste of time or that planning and budgeting *would never work in our organization*. However, these same managers have at least some hidden ideas about what they want to accomplish. But if they cannot articulate and communicate these thoughts (and plans) to others in the organization, the only way the organization will ever accomplish its desired goals and objectives is by accident. Some of these organizations may even be successful to a degree in terms of sales and profits; but, they could probably be even more successful with effective use of the planning and budgeting process.

Some of the advantages, to an organization, of a budgeting process are that it

a. requires managers to plan;

b. enhances communication of plans throughout the organization;

c. reduces doubts about what each manager needs to do—and how it is to be done;

d. requires managers to think ahead by necessitating formalization of their plans;

e. provides specific goals and objectives which serve as benchmarks for subsequent evaluation of results achieved;

f. identifies potential constraints or trouble spots before problems occur;

g. coordinates organizational activities by integrating plans and objectives of the functional disciplines; and

h. ensures that plans and objectives are consistent with organizational goals.

Budget Pitfalls

Employee attitudes toward the budget are based in large part on the budget development process as well as top management's attitude toward budgeting in general. To be successful, the budget process must have senior management's support. The budget should not be used in the following ways:

- As a *hammer* or punitive tool: Finding someone to blame when things go wrong.
- As an operational straitjacket: Giving minimum freedom to operating management or conferring absolute control to senior management.
- As an excuse for inaction: *I can't do it; it's not in the budget!*
- As a pot of funds that must be spent: All budgeted funds should have a specific purpose related to appropriate goals and objectives; and if money is not spent during the budget period that should not be the reason for deleting the funds from future budgets.

- For playing budget *games* such as high and low negotiating,
  hoarding, creating funds cushions, making targets too easy
  to be meaningful or too hard to be attainable, managerial
  harassment, or *gotchas.*

The budget should be used as a positive force to assist the organization in
establishing expectations, measuring results, working toward corporate goals
and objectives, and identifying operational areas in need of improvement.

The Budgeting Process

Structure of the Master Budget

The master budget contains two major parts:

1. The operating budget, reflecting the results of operating decisions,
   and
2. The financial budget depicting the financial outcomes.

The operating budget consists of various pieces such as

- sales budget, including sales forecast and expected cash receipts;
- production budget, including production schedule and inventory plans;
- manufacturing budget, including material, labor, and manufacturing overhead costs;
- selling costs budget;
- general and administrative costs budget;
- budgeted income statement prepared in normal financial reporting or contribution analysis format.

The financial budget normally consists of

- cash budget;
- budgeted (pro forma) balance sheet;
- capital budget;
- R&D and other project-oriented budgets.

Preparing the Operating Budget

The major steps in preparing the operating budget are to

- prepare a sales forecast;
- determine production volume necessary to support the sales forecast and inventory requirements;
- estimate manufacturing and support costs at the determined level of production.

This is followed by the financial budgeting process which

- projects cash flow and other financial effects and needs;
- estimates capital investment requirements for the period and generates a capital budget;
- prepares any required project budgets;
- develops pro forma financial statements from the prior list.

The Sales Budget

The entire budget activity is driven principally by the sales forecast. Unless you can forecast the level of sales, you really cannot plan the level of production and operations and related costs. The sales forecasting process can be schematically depicted as follows:

Strategic objectives
Market projections
Department plans
Resource constraints = Sales forecast

The sales budget normally shows the quantity and dollar value of each product or service expected to be sold or delivered. Some of the methods for estimating the sales budget include

a. a statistical forecast based on an analysis of general business conditions, market conditions, competitive situation, and so forth;

b. internal estimates based on input and opinions of management and sales personnel

c. analysis of factors affecting sales revenue and then *prediction* of future behavior of these factors.

Once sales volume has been estimated, the sales budget can be developed by multiplying estimated volume in units by expected unit sales price, as shown in the following table.

Sales budget

	A	B	C	D	Total
Expected unit sales	2,200	6,800	12,100	8,400	29,500
Unit sales price	$125	$60	$30	$80	
Total budget sales	$275,000	$408,000	$363,000	$672,000	$1,718,000

Sales Forecasts

The sales forecast is one of the primary inputs into the business planning process. Not only is it necessary to know what was sold in the past and to whom and at what price and profit margin, but also to know what the company is going to sell in the future. It is this future sales forecast that the business will use to develop its planned profit plan. This becomes the sales budget on which it plans its production budget of goods and services—taking into account what already exists in inventory—and with accurate and realistic costs, its profit plan, and cash budget. The greater the number of real customer orders in the sales budget, the more accurate the profit plan will be. With inaccuracies and guesstimates based on prior year's inaccurate sales forecasts in the current sales forecast, the business will produce or purchase more for inventory than for customers, which will in turn result in failure to meet its profit plan and an unfavorable cash position. Management together with sales personnel must play an integral role to formulate accurate sales forecasts upon which to establish controls to monitor and evaluate against.

The sales forecast amounts compared to actual sales for the past year for products A, B, and C are shown in the following chart.

Sales forecast to actual sales

Product	Forecast	Sales	Difference	%
A	800	540	260	32.5
B	12,000	9,800	2,200	18.3
C	3,600	2,200	1,400	38.8

Analysis of this chart shows that the sales forecast is way out of line for all three products, but is closest for Product B. With such a sales forecast, it is quite difficult for the business to plan effectively. It is apparent that the business must have more realistic sales forecasts in order to plan their operations and expected results. This usually means that the sales staff must get closer to their customers. The business must be able to establish realistic sales goals for each product (or product line) in order to direct the sales function and plan their internal operations.

THE SALES FORECAST COMES FROM YOUR CUSTOMERS NOT FROM YOUR SALES FORCE

Although maintaining sales statistics by product and customer is important, management must learn how to analyze and interpret what these numbers really mean. For instance, it must identify the customers to whom it is selling products A, B, and C, and determine how these customers are purchasing—that is, strictly by ordering on their own, through the business's sales direction, from its catalog, and so on. In effect, the business must define the relationship of past sales to future forecasts: Will they increase, stay about the same, or decrease, and to what extent? It is only through the sales function that the business can determine this needed information. For the business, the task of establishing more accurate sales forecasts, effective sales reporting systems and controls, and evaluation and corrective action procedures normally falls upon management. The business needs to move toward more realistic sales forecasts in which the largest proportion possible (e.g., 80 percent or more) is made up of real customer orders. In this manner, management can develop realistic sales, production, cost, pricing, and profit plans working with the sales function to make the plan happen. An effective organizational planning system is the tool to make this happen.

| SALES TEND TO BE OVERESTIMATED |
| IN THE PLANNING PROCESS |

The Production Budget

After the sales budget has been completed, the production budget can be prepared. The production budget establishes the number of units expected to be produced and the related inventory requirements to meet the sales budget. The expected volume of production is determined by subtracting the estimated inventory at the beginning of the period from the sum of the units expected to be sold and the desired inventory at the end of the period.

For example:

Production budget

	A	B	C	D	Total
Planned sales	2,200	6,800	12,100	8,400	29,500
Planned ending inventory (10% of annual sales)	220	680	1,210	840	2,950
Total requirements	2,420	7,480	13,310	9,240	32,450
Less beginning inventory	180	740	1,060	980	2,960
Production budget (production units)	2,240	6,740	12,250	8,260	29,490

Manufacturing Cost Budgets

Based on the production budget, manufacturing cost budgets can be developed for direct material, direct labor, and manufacturing overhead. The *direct material budget* is based on the amount of material that must be purchased to meet production requirements and desired inventory levels. The method for calculating the amount of material purchases is to multiply the production budget requirements by the number of each purchased part required by its respective cost.

If product A from the previous table requires two widgets at $3.50, six T-rings at 50¢, and five electristors at $1.75, the material budget would be: 4,480 widgets at $3.50 ($15,680), plus 13,440 T-rings at 50¢ ($6,720), and 11,200 electristors at $1.75 ($19,600) or a total of

$42,000. Any adjustment to the inventory of the widgets, electristors, and T-rings would also have to be figured into the calculation as would any anticipated price changes. Similar calculations must then be made for each other product produced to arrive at an overall purchases budget for direct materials.

For example, the following purchasing plan can be used:

Purchasing plan

	Unit Cost $	A	B	C	D	Total $
Widgets	3.50	2	–	–	2	73,500
T-rings	0.50	6	6	3	–	45,315
Electristors	1.75	5	1	2	–	74,270
Gizmos	2.00	–	3	–	1	56,960
Arclets	0.12	–	20	2	–	19,116
Links	0.35	–	–	–	5	14,455
No. of production units		2,240	6,740	12,250	8,260	
$ purchases		$42,000	$88,631	$64,190	$88,795	$283,616
$/unit		18.75	13.15	5.24	10.75	

Direct labor requirements are calculated by multiplying the expected production volume by the number of direct labor hours needed to produce a unit and then multiplying the result by the hourly labor rate paid. In the case of product A in the aforementioned table, if it takes 2.1 hours to produce the part and the labor rate is $8.50 per hour, the labor budget would be 2,240 units × 2.1 hours = 4,704 hours × $8.50/hour = $39,984. As in the case of direct material purchases, similar calculations must be made for other items produced to arrive at an overall direct labor budget.

For example, the following labor plan can be used:

Labor plan

	A	B	C	D	Total
Labor hours/unit	2.10	0.95	0.30	1.80	
× labor rate/hour	$8.50	$8.00	$8.60	$6.50	
× # production units	2,240	6,740	12,250	8,260	
= direct labor $	$39,984	$51,224	$31,605	$96,642	$219,455
Direct labor $/unit	17.85	7.60	2.58	11.70	

In the case of direct material and direct labor budgets, changes in product mix can significantly alter the numbers. A large shift from a material-intensive to a labor-intensive product will have a major impact on the relative amounts of material and labor costs. The same phenomenon will occur if the organization shifts from in-house manufacturing to sending work outside or vice versa.

Manufacturing overhead costs budgets involve development of estimates of costs for all manufacturing costs other than direct material and direct labor. These budget estimates must be built up on an account-by-account basis so that accurate budget figures will be calculated for both planning and control purposes.

An example of a simplified manufacturing overhead budget for our company follows:

Production salaries	$180,400
Depreciation	$79,300
Fringe benefits	$53,900
Utilities	$35,900
Supplies	$30,600
Misc. other costs	$58,900
Total mfg. overhead	$439,000 (or 200% of direct labor)

Operating Costs Budgets

Selling costs and general and administrative costs budgets are estimates of the amounts that will be required to sell the product or service and to carry on the general administrative activities that are necessary to support the entire organization. They are normally budgeted on a line-by-line basis similar to the manufacturing overhead costs described earlier.

An example of an operating costs budget for our company follows:

Commissions—4.0% of sales	$ 68,720
Misc. variable selling costs	$93,000
Advertising	$40,000
Sales salaries	$95,000
Other selling expenses	$12,480
Total selling expenses	$ 309,200

(Contiuned)

G and A salaries	$ 95,000
Rent	$75,000
Insurance	$20,000
Office supplies	$20,500
Misc. other G and A expenses	$4,400
Total G and A expenses	$224,900
Total budgeted selling and G and A expenses	$ 534,100

COSTS TEND TO BE UNDERESTIMATED IN THE PLANNING PROCESS

Budgeted Income Statement

The budgeted income statement summarizes the projections of revenues and expenses for the budgeting period. Note that direct material, dirt labor, and manufacturing overhead figures are based on products sold, not produced, according to the following table:

Projections of Revenues and Expenses

	Budgeted sales	Material unit cost $	Material budget $	Labor unit cost $	Labor budget $
Product A	2,200	18.75	41,250	17.85	39,270
Product B	6,800	13.15	89,420	7.60	51,680
Product C	12,100	5.24	63,404	2.58	31,218
Product D	8,400	10.75	90,300	11.70	98,280
Total			$284,374		$220,448

Beginning and ending inventory figures are calculated as follows:

Beginning and Ending Inventory Calculations

	Beginning inventory			Ending inventory		
	# Units	Cost	Inv. $	# Units	Cost	Inv. $
Product A	180	$72.05	$12,969	220	$72.30	$15,906
Product B	740	35.56	$26,314	680	35.95	$24,446
Product C	1,060	12.80	$13,568	1,210	12.98	$15,706
Product D	980	46.50	$45,570	840	45.85	$38,514
Total			$98,421			$94,572

The budgeted income statement for our company can thus be presented as follows:

Budgeted income statement

Sales	$1,718,000
Less cost of goods sold:	
Beginning inventory (2,960 units)	$ 98,400
Direct material	$284,400
Direct labor	$220,400
Mfg. overhead (200% of direct labor)	$440,800
Ending inventory (2,950 units)	$(94,600)
Total cost of goods sold	$949,400
Manufacturing profit	**$768,600**
Less operating costs	
Selling expenses	$309,200
G & A expenses	$224,900
Total selling, G & A expenses	$534,100
Operating profit before taxes	$234,500
Interest expense	$43,500
Profit before income taxes	$191,000
Taxes at 30%	$57,300
Net income	$ 133,700

Financial Budgets

a. Pro forma balance sheet: The pro forma balance sheet is developed by starting with the balance sheet for the year previously ended, and then adjusting it based on all of the planned activities for the current budgeting period. Some benefits of preparing a pro forma balance sheet include the following:

- To disclose a possibly unfavorable financial condition
- To provide a final verification of the accuracy of all the other budgets
- To allow for the calculation of financial ratios
- To highlight future resource needs and constraints

As an example, let's look at the following beginning balance sheet of our company:

Beginning balance sheet

Assets		Liabilities and equity	
Cash	$77,500	Accounts payable and accruals	$96,620
Accounts receivable	$184,100	Income taxes payable	$21,980
Inventory	$98,400	Total current liabilities	$118,600
Total current assets	$360,000	Long-term debt	$510,000
		Total liabilities	$628,600
Land	$750,000		
Buildings and equipment	$1,312,500	Common stock	$500,000
Accumulated depreciation	$(812,500)	Retained earnings	$481,400
Total fixed assets	$1,250,000	*Total shareholders equity*	$981,400
Total assets	$1,610,000	Total liabilities and equity	$1,610,000

By using the information in the budget sections discussed previously and including some assumptions regarding other aspects of the balance sheet not presented, we can develop the following balance sheet to represent the ending position of our example company:

Ending balance sheet

Assets		Liabilities and equity	
Cash	$133,700	Accounts payable and accruals	$145,020
Accounts receivable	$264,600	Income taxes payable	$26,480
Inventory	$94,600	*Total current liabilities*	$171,500
Total current assets	$492,900	Long-term debt	$472,000
		Total liabilities	$643,500
Land	$750,000		
Buildings and equipments	$1,407,500	Common stock	$500,000
Accumulated depreciation	$(891,800)	Retained earnings	$615,100
Total fixed assets	$1,265,700	*Total shareholders equity*	$1,115,100
Total assets	$1,758600	Total liabilities and equity	$1,758,600

From this set of financial information, company management has the ability to review its projected financial status and determine what if anything needs to be done to provide for problems or emergencies; or what opportunities can be taken advantage of to most effectively utilize the company's financial strengths.

b. Cash Budget: The cash budget is prepared for the purpose of cash planning and control and represents the expected cash inflow and outflow for the designated time period. It helps management to maintain cash balances in a reasonable relationship to its needs. It also aids in planning for and even sometimes avoiding unnecessary idle cash and cash shortages. The cash budget usually consists of the following elements:

- Operating activities: All cash transactions that are not classified as investing or financing activities.
- Investing activities: Cash receipts and disbursements for investment activities such as securities that are not cash equivalents, productive assets with extended lives, or loans made to others.
- Financing activities: Borrowings and loan repayments anticipated during the time period or equity transactions

For example, for our company:

Cash flows from (for) operating activities

Net income	$133,700
Adjustments to reconcile net income to cash flows from operating activities	
Depreciation	$79,300
Changes in assets and liabilities	
Increase in accounts receivable	$(80,500)
Decrease in inventories	$3,800
Increase in accounts payable and accruals	$48,400
Increase in income taxes payable	$4,500
Net cash generated from (for) operations	$189,200
Cash flows from (for) investing activities	
Capital equipment	$(95,000)
Cash flows from (for) financing activities	
New borrowing	$250,000
Debt repayment	$(288,000)
Net cash generated from (for) financing	$(38,000)
Total cash generated	$56,200
Beginning cash balance	$77,500
Ending cash balance	$ 133,700

Budgeting Applications

Developing the Budget

The chances for success of the organization's budget program is determined in large part by the method used to develop the budget. Normally, the most successful budget programs are those that allow managers (and other appropriate operations personnel) who have the responsibility for related operating costs to prepare their own budgets based on agreed upon overall organizational goals and objectives. This bottom-up budgeting method can be very effective if, as is usually the case, the budget is to be used subsequently to control the manager's operations. For if the budget is developed by upper management and then enforced entirely by management directive, it will most likely be resented, and will foster animosity toward rather than cooperation with upper management.

When managers (and their staffs) prepare their own budgets, they have invested more in making the results work and feel more supportive toward the budget goals. These *self-imposed* or participative budgets have other advantages, such as

a. recognition of staff input at all organizational levels, creating more of a *working-together* atmosphere;

b. feeling by personnel that their input is valued by top management, and that they can make some of their own decisions;

c. more accurate and reliable budget estimates since those actually involved in the operation can normally make better estimates;

d. a greater likelihood that individuals will work toward the budget objectives if they have been involved in preparing the budget themselves as opposed to dealing with the previously imposed budget;

e. the creation of a situation where, if budget is not met, the preparers can only blame themselves; whereas, with the previously imposed budgets, the individuals tend to blame others—for example, budget was unreasonable, unrealistic, impossible to meet, and so forth;

f. even self-imposed budgets will be reviewed and approved by upper management. But if changes are necessary they can be discussed and acceptable compromises reached. In this type of budget system, all levels of the organization work together to produce the budget, but since upper management is typically less familiar with day-to-day operations, they rely on operational management and staff to provide necessary detailed budget data. On the other hand, top management is more aware of the broader organizational goals and objectives (and desired directions) and can provide vital input to the budget process to help coordinate the overall needs of the business. The budget process, then, becomes one where each organizational level cooperates with the others to develop a fully integrated plan of action;

Flexible Budgets

The budgets thus far reviewed, that is, sales, production, cash, and so forth, presume a single level of activity and are static. A flexible budget, on the other hand, assumes a range of activity and is dynamic. Ideally, a series of budgets should be developed for various levels of operating activity. The primary use of flexible budgeting is to measure performance accurately by comparing actual costs for a given level of output with budgeted costs for the same activity level. The key to developing the flexible budget is identifying and isolating the variable costs that move proportionately with changes in levels of operating activity from fixed costs, which change independently from changes in activity levels or remain unchanged during the budget period.

Following are examples that show differences in results using *static* as compared to *flexible* budgeting. In the first example, static budgeting is used to show two divisions of a company that manufacture and sell a similar product. Note that division A's sales are below budget, while division B's sales exceed budget. In this example, actual results are compared to the original budget that has not been adjusted to reflect the actual volume achieved. Thus, it appears that division A is $25,000 (7 percent) under budget in gross profit while division B has exceeded its gross profit budget by $86,000 or almost 25 percent.

Manufacturing budget report-static

	Division A			Division B		
	Budget	**Actual**	**Variance**	**Budget**	**Actual**	**Variance**
Units produced	20,000	18,000	(2,000)	20,000	24,000	4,000
Sales	$1,000	$940	($60)	$1,000	$1,152	$152
Costs:						
Material	$200	$190	$10	$200	$225	$(25)
Direct labor	$140	$130	$10	$140	$160	$(20)
Variable overhead	$135	$125	$10	$135	$158	$(23)
Fixed overhead	$175	$170	$5	$175	$173	$2
Total costs	$650	$615	$35	$650	$716	$(66)
Gross profit	$350	$325	($25)	$350	$436	$86

As no company conducts its operations totally according to its plan and budget, as planned activities change so must the corresponding budget. Thus, planning and budgeting are ongoing ever-changing processes. A reflecting budget change based on activity changes is known as flexible budgeting. The budgets thus far discussed, that is, sales, production, cash, and so forth, presume a single level of activity and are thus static in nature. A flexible budget, on the other hand, recognizes the probability of a range of activities and is dynamic in nature. It is possible to develop a series of budgets for various levels of activities. The primary use of flexible budgeting is to measure performance accurately by comparing actual costs for a given level of output with budgeted costs for the same activity level. An example of a flexible budget for the same manufacturing operations is shown next.

In this example, revenues and variable costs have been adjusted proportionately to reflect the change in actual sales volume from budget—in other words a flexible budget. Fixed costs, of course, have not been adjusted. Our analysis now shows an entirely different result than the prior example using static budgeting. Using the flexible budgeting approach, division B is below budget in gross profit by $19,000 (4 percent) and division A has exceeded its gross profit budget by $28,000 (9 percent).

Manufacturing budget report—flexible

	Division A			Division B		
	Budget	Actual	Variance	Budget	Actual	Variance
Units produced	20,000	18,000	(2,000)	20,000	24,000	4,000
Sales	$900	$940	$40	$1,200	$1,152	($48)
Costs:						
Material	$180	$190	$(10)	$240	$225	$15
Direct labor	$126	$130	$(4)	$168	$160	$8
Variable overhead	$122	$125	$(3)	$162	$158	$4
Fixed overhead	$175	$170	$5	$175	$173	$2
Total costs	$603	$615	$(12)	$745	$716	$29
Gross profit	$297	$325	$28	$455	$436	($19)

Further analysis reveals that division A has achieved its favorable profitability variance through effective pricing of product and that cost control is in need of attention. Division B shows the opposite—effective cost control, but less effective pricing. These two examples depict how the use of flexible budgeting can provide management with the information necessary to make such analyses. This in turn can provide direction for management to address areas requiring attention in the sales and manufacturing functions.

Budgeting for Nonmanufacturing Organizations

Nonmanufacturing firms—retailers, wholesalers, service providers, and so forth—have just as critical a need for effective planning and budgeting as do manufacturing organizations. However, the budgeting process is not normally as complex. As in the case of a manufacturing organization, a nonmanufacturer's budgeting process starts with a sales forecast or estimate of revenues. Although nonmanufacturers may not be concerned with such things as raw materials, direct labor, or manufacturing overhead, they may be concerned with the purchase of merchandise for resale and provision of labor-intensive services. The amount of these purchases and costs of labor are, obviously, related to expected sales or revenues and must be budgeted accordingly. The nonmanufacturers' preparation of the budget for operating expenses is very similar to the manufacturing organization. The resultant budget package provides management with the same quality of information for planning, controlling, and evaluating the results of their operations that exists in a manufacturing environment.

An example of a static and flexible line item type budget for a service organization is shown as follows:

Service organization: Line item budget—static budget report

	Budget	Actual	Better (worse) than budget
Revenues:			
Units of service	600	540	$(1,800)
Average charge per hour	$30	$26	$(2,160)
Total revenues	$18,000	$14,040	$(3,960)
Expenses:			
Personnel	$13,968	$12,440	$1,528
Materials and supplies	$767	$1,682	$(915)
Rent	$500	$500	$0
Utilities	$667	$783	$(116)
Insurance	$300	$1,460	$(1,160)
Transportation	$100	$180	$(80)
Contracted services	$50	$400	$(350)
Other expenses	$60	$12	$48
Total expenses	$16,412	$17,457	$(1,045)
Excess of revenues over (under) expenses	*$1,588*	*$(3,417)*	*$(5,005)*

Service organization: Line item budget—flexible budget report

	Original budget	Adjusted budget	Actual	Better (worse) than budget
Revenues:				
Units of service	600	540	540	0
Average charge per hour	$30	$30	$26	$(2,160)
Total revenues	$18,000	$16,200	$14,040	$(2,160)

(*Continued*)

Expenses:				
Personnel	$13,968	$12,351	$12,440	$(89)
Materials and supplies	$767	$690	$1,682	$(992)
Rent	$500	$500	$500	$0
Utilities	$667	$600	$783	$(183)
Insurance	$300	$243	$1,460	$(1,217)
Transportation	$100	$90	$180	$(90)
Contracted services	$50	$400	$400	$0
Other expenses	$60	$12	$12	$0
Total expenses	$16,412	$14,886	$17,457	$(2,571)
Excess of revenues over (under) expenses	$1,588	$1,314	$(3,417)	$(4,731)

Line-Item Budgeting

Some organizations, particularly those in the nonprofit or the public sector, are more likely to budget on the basis of cash flows (receipts and expenditures) as opposed to revenues and expenses. The budgeting process may start with expenditures rather than with receipts—in effect, the budgeting problem becomes one of determining the amount of receipts required to support the level of expenditures desired or perceived necessary to carry out the organizations mission. This is the reverse of the more typical budgeting situation discussed earlier where revenues are the principal driving force in the budgeting process, and costs necessary to support the forecast level of activity are calculated subsequently.

An expenditure-driven budgeting process normally lends itself to a *line item* type of budget, with standard line item expenses (e.g., personnel, fringe benefits, materials and supplies, equipment, etc.) for each unit within the organization that expends funds. These budgets normally require line-by-line expenditure submission and approval. Due to line item budget constraints, this type of budgeting system often prevents managers from exercising their discretion in using budgeted funds to achieve stated goals and objectives. Many times managers are not allowed to increase spending on a line item even though they may be able to make corresponding decreases on other line items. This inflexibility can produce actions that may be inconsistent with organizational objectives or even good common sense and business judgment. The inherent problem with line-item budgeting is the emphasis on individual expense items and types of costs as opposed to concentration on objectives to be accomplished.

Another concern with line-item budgeting is its tendency to encourage current budget setting based on prior years' (usually last year or an average of the past few years) budgets or actual expenses for each line item. This type of budgeting methodology is known as incremental budgeting. Using this technique, an operating unit may be allowed a 5 or 10 percent increase (or forced toward a 5 or 10 percent decrease) in the budgeted line item(s). Or sometimes top management may grant an overall budget increase and then allow departments to use the total increase for whatever line items they desire. These options do not adequately focus on the achievement of objectives or the differences among line items. Also, this type of budgeting may foster budgeting manipulation such as

- spending up to the budgeted line item's limit, whether the full amount is necessary or not—creating unnecessary expenditures this year to justify a bigger budget for next year;
- end of year *panic* purchases to ensure the expenditure of the full budget allotment so that no money will be taken away from the following year's budget amount;
- use of the budget as a status symbol (the larger the budget, the more powerful the department and the individual manager);
- assuming that overall budget approval by top management means blanket spending approval for each line item.

Zero-Based Budgeting

Zero-based budgeting is a management planning and budgeting tool that directs managers to justify budget requests in their entirety. While line item budgeting emphasizes incremental changes from the previous year and assumes that previous year's activities are essential and must be continued, zero-based budgeting requires budget requests to be developed essentially from a zero base—that is, disregarding completely prior year activity levels—and justified completely for the current period. Under this approach, each manager must convince higher management that the current budget request and related purpose is necessary and is a more critical need for organizational resources than other departmental requests. Such justification is done through a series of decision packages in which the departmental manager ranks all the departmental activities as to relative importance, from the top ranking of those activities that are considered essential to those of least importance that might be *nice to do*. This approach then allows upper management to evaluate each decision package independently so that they can approve those activities that are considered most significant and cost justified and reduce, or eliminate, those activities considered unnecessary or not cost justified. In addition, it allows top management to allocate overall organizational financial resources across departmental lines based on criteria of need and justification. The goals of zero based budgeting are to make sure that specific activities (and their related expenditures) are still needed and that such expenditures are being made most economically as related to the activities' effectiveness.

Program Budgeting

The concept of program budgeting is to apply the budgeting process to an overall program or general purpose—or focus on why the funds need to be spent rather than on how funds are to be specifically spent. Program budgeting emphasizes the desired end results (reasons for the program) and measures the total cost of the program over several years rather than just the first year's costs. It forces choices among program alternatives and creates competition for allocation of capital resources. Budgeting by program normally allows top management to make better decisions about the use and allocation of financial resources. The program budgeting concept also enables departmental managers to determine various levels of services and related levels of expenditures. This feature is somewhat similar to zero-based budgeting. Program budgets that specify goals and objectives (results) clearly allow management to see where their money is going and subsequently to determine if it was spent effectively. Program budgeting (and zero-based budgeting) is most commonly found in the public sector (i.e., government, school districts, social service agencies, etc.). However, their principles can be just as applicable to business entities. For example, businesses have been increasingly concerned with productivity, and many have adopted variations of these budgeting techniques to address productivity issues. As a result, program and zero-based budgets are sometimes developed by business in addition to the more traditional type budgets.

Differences Between Planning and Budgeting

Planning

1. Sets goals and objectives
2. Determines basic policy decisions
3. Establishes programs
4. Is more general than budgeting
5. Identifies output desired

Budgeting

1. Analyzes input and resources required
2. Analyzes in detail functions or activities to implement each program
3. Allows analysis of alternatives within each activity to achieve results desired, and
4. Identifies trade-offs between partial and complete achievement of established goals and associated costs.

Budgeting Considerations

Budgeting is

1. a control of the financial activities of the organization;
2. a device to create a plan of action—organization's blueprint in dollar terms—must know the organization and its goals and objectives before preparation of budget;
3. a financial plan of action based on plans for future;
4. A tool to monitor dollars during the operating period (income, expenses, and expenditures);
5. a managerial program that serves to reflect the objectives of management, which objectives must be known by all levels of management in order to properly prepare the budget;

6. a technique to allocate resources and coordinate management activities to achieve the best overall results from the plans made;

7. the connecting link between the plan and actual performance as recorded in the accounting records and reports; and

8. not a substitute for good business judgment.

Budgeting Objectives

1. To provide a written expression, in quantitative terms, of the plans and policies of the organization.

2. To provide a basis for the evaluation of financial performance in accordance with the plans, and

3. To provide a useful method for controlling revenues and expenses.

Rules of Good Budgeting

The budget should be

1. well-conceived and approved by appropriate staff personnel;

2. divided into meaningful measurement periods;

3. periodically compared to actual results for corrective action, replanning, and decision-making purposes;

4. flexible so that appropriate action can be taken based on results of operations or adjustments can be made to reflect changing environmental conditions.

5. joint effort of many people, creating a working document that forms the basis for action.

Budgeting Assumptions

The budget should be

1. realistic and attainable;

2. based on relevant internal and external factors;

3. set up to offer alternative choices in detail;

4. formal, clearly understood, and conclusive for easy control;

5. expressed in financial or relevant quantitative terms;

6. focused on the individuals who are responsible for implementation.

Prerequisites

1. Set of well-defined policies and objectives
2. Sound organizational structure
3. Involvement of all levels of management
4. Functionally classified accounting system
5. Presence of a responsibility accounting system
6. Accumulation of adequate, accurate, and relevant historical data
7. Formal reporting system

Byproducts

1. Provides basis for reassessing existing organization relationships, goals, objectives, and services.
2. Enhances preplanning, cooperation, and effectiveness among the management group.
3. Makes management, at all levels, aware of constraints on revenues, expenses, and cash.
4. Enhances awareness of detail and thoroughness in follow-up and value of historical information and its use in the planning process.
5. Checks on the progress in achieving objectives, especially if management by objectives (MBO) system is in place.
6. Establishes clearer definition of organizational relationships and identification of authority and responsibility.
7. Analyzes external and internal environmental factors.

Steps in Budgeting

1. Set goals and establish objectives, and develop resulting action plans.
2. Allocate resources and costs of action plans.
3. Project income to evaluate sources of revenues and timing of cash flows.
4. Allocate income based on budget results and action plans.

5. Develop participation and involvement to the lowest organizational level possible, and

6. Use budget results for decision making.

> ## THE BUDGET IS THE DOLLAR VALUE
> ## OF ACHIEVING RESULTS

CHAPTER 5

Management Reporting and Control

It is the purpose of this chapter to show the elements involved in closing the loop on the overall strategic and long-range planning, short-term planning, and budgeting process and how these techniques can be used to enhance the probability of achieving organizational goals and objectives. To accomplish this effectively, the organization needs to implement accurate and timely reporting systems so that management can control the execution of the planning and budgeting process, and take timely action to fix the cause of any problems or concerns, so that they do not occur again. In addition, management needs to know what is working well, so that they can make necessary changes to take advantage of these situations.

The objectives of this chapter are to

1. discuss the principal elements of control for the organization;
2. introduce the concept of responsibility accounting and responsibility centers as it relates to effective reporting and control techniques;
3. to introduce some concepts for cost center performance evaluation such as variance reporting;
4. to discuss profit center performance evaluation techniques;
5. to identify report concepts, features, and techniques;
6. develop some of the methods of evaluating the performance of the organization and its segments; and
7. review the importance of reporting during the feedback process, and to discuss some of the better (and weak) aspects of reporting financial information.

**PLANS ARE EVER CHANGING
AND NEED TO BE MONITORED**

In previous chapters, we discussed various methods and techniques for gathering and reporting information within the organization. We have also identified how important it is for management to use accounting related information to plan and control internal operations. In this chapter, we will review these concepts in more depth. We will first look at the idea of control in general and then specifically examine the concept of *responsibility accounting*, a process that addresses evaluation of managerial performance. Finally, we will review the key elements of the reporting process.

Management Control

Management control has as one of its major objectives the organizational development of goal congruence, whereby managers and operating personnel work together toward meeting the organization's, department's, and function's goals and objectives—and not just their own personal goals and objectives. To do this effectively, employees must have some incentive to work toward organizational goals. Management's task is to create an environment in which employees can motivate themselves to work toward these organizational goals. An effective management accounting and reporting system can help provide such a positive atmosphere. Inasmuch as managers will be evaluating those reporting to them to a substantial degree on the basis of information that comes from management and the operations accounting system, it needs to be well designed for the purposes it is designed to attain and clearly understood by personnel who will be directly affected by it. A well designed operations accounting and reporting system should encompass at least the following principles:

- Show separately those factors which management can control and evaluate.
- Provide adequate feedback to the manager.
- Inform the manager about what has been happening, what trends might be expected, and, to the extent possible, the cause for the way they happened, and
- Highlight areas for attention and positive improvement.

For the management accounting and reporting system to be most effective, the managers and employees must trust it, and they must believe that it accurately portrays performance. In addition, managers must believe that the accounting and reporting system is fair. Thus, performance evaluation criteria that are used must be under the control of the managers and departments being evaluated. For the system to perform its function for the overall organization, the feedback provided and the criteria used for evaluation must provide a motivational environment for managers and employees to perform in a manner that moves them toward accomplishing their organizational goals and objectives.

An effective management control and reporting system is designed to provide meaningful and accurate information to management so that they can effectively manage those reporting to them and take necessary remedial action for necessary improvements in a program of continuous improvements—in effect, to help make the company a learning organization and to coach employees to become more effective.

Some other principles related to management and operations reporting and control include the following:

1. The planning, budgeting, and control process require top management support if it is to be effectively implemented.
2. Participation and involvement by those subject to control in setting control procedures will help gain acceptance and adherence much more quickly and positively than will unilateral imposition of controls and related systems.
3. Controls must be reasonable, understandable, appropriate, and fair to be acceptable to those responsible for compliance.
4. Budgets are to be used as planning and guidance tools—and not as punitive devices.
5. Variance analysis should be used to explain variations from plan, not to mete out blame or punishment. Finger pointing and defensive behavior does nothing to create more effective performance in the future. Also note that negative variances are not necessarily bad, nor are positive variances necessarily good—they must be examined in context.

Remember. It is *people*
who run the business and
determine success or failure,
not budgets or controls or financial ratios or variances or reports
or
other exclusively quantitative factors !

ONE IS ONLY RESPONSIBLE
FOR WHAT ONE HAS CONTROL OVER

Control

Control is the process used to monitor the organization's progress toward achieving its goals and objectives. Control involves collecting information, evaluating performance, and taking necessary corrective action. It is an activity that is an integral part of every manager's responsibility, whether or not the word *control* or *controller* manifests itself in the job title (i.e., controller, quality control manager, inventory control director, etc.). The management control and process loop is shown in Figure 5.1.

In order for the controlling process to actually happen, the following fundamental elements must be in place:

- Identification of standards: Corporate goals and objectives must be articulated in such a way that their achievement or lack thereof can be examined and analyzed.
- Performance measurement: Organizational performance must be measured to determine objectively and accurately what actual results are being achieved.
- Performance evaluation: Measurements must be made comparing actual performance against expectations to determine if the results achieved meet those expectations, and
- Reaction or response: Corrective action must be taken where results do not match expectations to bring performance up to standard, or to adjust standards to more realistic levels.

Each of these four elements is critical, and without any one of them the control process will not operate effectively.

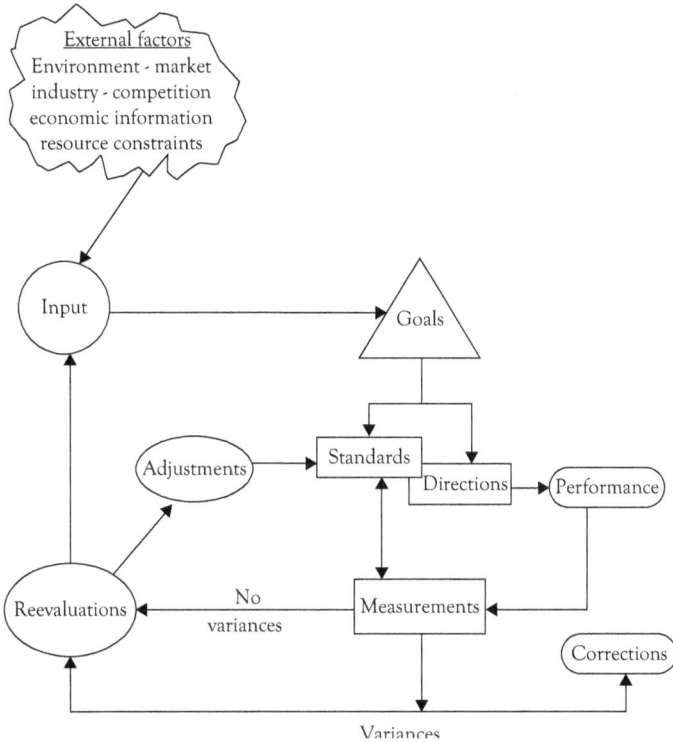

Figure 5.1 Management control process loop

CONTROL IS A HELPFUL SYSTEM
THAT KEEPS THE PLAN MOVING CORRECTLY

Responsibility Accounting

A responsibility accounting system assists in establishing standards of performance as yardsticks to measure against in an effective management evaluation and control system. Managerial performance evaluation allows for rewards to those who perform well and for the opportunity to take positive remedial action with those not performing up to expectations. Responsibility accounting pertains to the reporting of information that allows management to facilitate control of operations and evaluate related performance. It is the organization's system for collecting and reporting income and expense information by areas of responsibility. Under a responsibility accounting concept, managers are delegated decision-making authority and responsibility for those activities occurring within their areas of responsibility, or *responsibility centers*. These may be called departments, divisions, sections, units, or other names depending on the organization and how it is structured. Responsibility accounting operates under the principle that managers should be held responsible for their own performance and the performance of all activities within their responsibility centers. Some of the advantages to an organization of using a responsibility accounting system include the following:

- It facilitates delegation of authority and subsequent decision making.
- It enables management to implement planning and control concepts related to setting of goals and objectives, and subsequent evaluation of progress toward such objectives.
- It establishes standards of performance to be used for comparison and evaluation purposes.
- It provides criteria for performance evaluation, and
- It allows for effective use of *management by exception* principles, whereby management's attention is focused on important variances from standards.

For a responsibility accounting system to be most effective, the following criteria within the organization should be considered at the front end:

- A defined organization structure, with management responsibility or authority relationships explicitly identified and unquestionably understood at all organizational levels.
- Clearly prescribed standards of performance related to income, expenditures, and operational activities.
- Managerial responsibilities (areas to be held accountable for) to include only those items that are controllable by the relevant manager(s).
- Performance reporting that highlights only those items requiring management attention. This management by exception concept directs management effort toward exceptional or problem situations or significant deviations from the plan and avoids unnecessary time spent reviewing results that meet established standards of performance.

RESPONSIBILITY AND ACCOUNTABILITY	
RELATE TO WHAT IS UNDER ONE'S CONTROL	

Responsibility Centers

A responsibility center within the organization is a unit having responsibility for and control over a specific, identifiable segment of the organization's activities. There are generally four types of responsibility centers:

a. Revenue center: A unit responsible for generating revenues. Examples might be a sales rep facility, a distributor organization, or other independently operated sales facility. While not a commonly used responsibility center, it might be appropriate if there is a revenue generating responsibility, which should be monitored. Variance analyses measuring quantity of units sold and revenue generated on a per unit basis compared to budgets or other pre-established standards would be relevant measures of performance for a revenue center.

b. Cost center: A unit measured by costs incurred. Cost centers do not generate revenue directly. Examples include quality control, maintenance, accounting, personnel, and so forth. Variance analyses based on comparisons of actual results to standard costs or flexible budgets would be typical performance measures for a cost center.

c. Profit center: A unit that generates revenues and is held responsible for the revenues earned and related costs that it incurs. Management typically is held accountable for the amount of profits earned. Examples include a sales division, a retail department, a loan unit in a bank, or other independent profit generating entity. Profit dollars, profit as a percent of revenues, or the contribution margin approach are widely used measures of performance for profit centers.

f. Investment center: A unit responsible for earning a rate of return on the investment in the unit (usually operating assets). For instance, major segments of an organization (strategic business units, operating divisions, individual retail outlets, branch offices, etc.) which are held responsible for the costs and revenues as well as the investment required to finance and operationally support the unit are logical candidates to be handled as investment centers. Return on

Functional organization structure

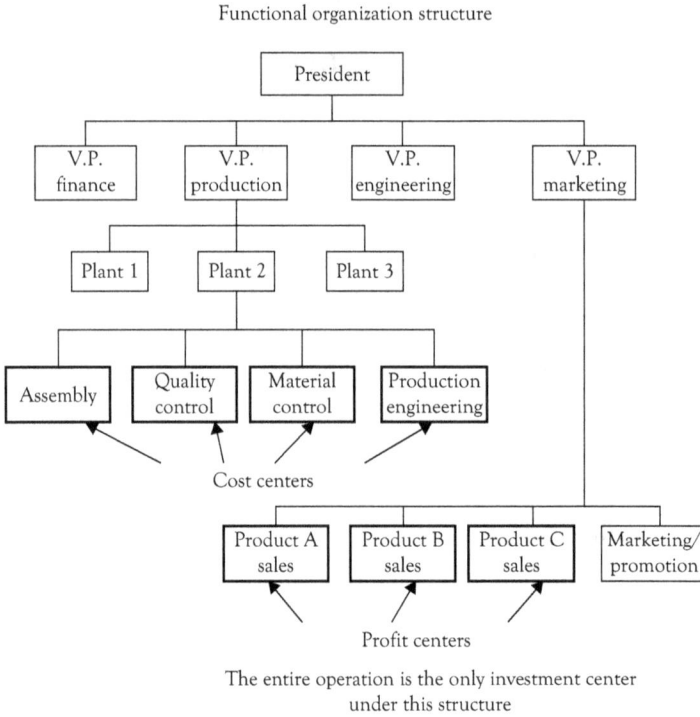

Figure 5.2 Cost and profit centers

investment (ROI) measures is the principal means of evaluating performance, although residual income (RI) (to be discussed later) is another method of evaluation that has relevance for an investment center. Cost and profit centers are depicted in Figure 5.2.

Investment centers differ from profit centers in that the former is evaluated on the basis of the return earned on investment in the center, while the latter is evaluated on the excess of revenues over expenses for the time period being measured. Recognize that an operating unit earning a larger amount of profit than another operating unit is not necessarily doing better—it may simply have a larger investment in assets with which to earn a larger profit. Therefore, it is generally preferable to designate a unit as an investment center rather than a profit center to increase the benefits of responsibility accounting and reporting and to take into account the existence of the investment base in addition to the revenue, expense,

Product organization structure

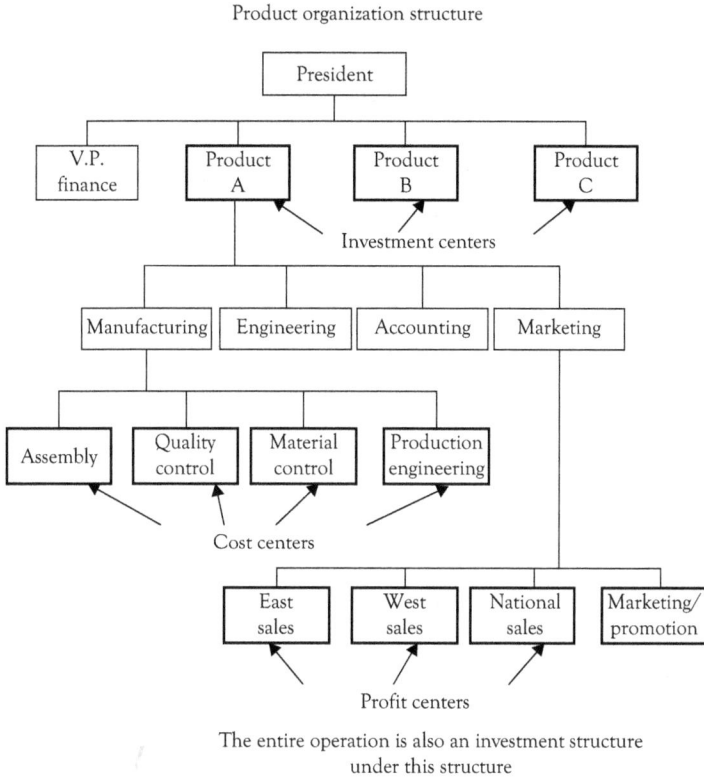

Figure 5.3 Cost, profit, and investment centers

and profitability figures. The relationship of cost, profit and investment centers is shown in Figure 5.3.

Cost Center Performance Evaluation

A major tool for measuring or evaluating the performance of a cost center is variance analysis, or analyzing the differences between budgeted (or standard) costs and actual costs incurred. For expenses, a variance is unfavorable if actual (cost or quantity) exceeds standard (cost or quantity). An expense variance is favorable if actual (cost or quantity) is less than standard (cost or quantity). For revenues the reverse is true—a favorable variance means more revenue (higher price or greater quantity) was received than was budgeted, and an unfavorable variance means less revenue than budget was generated.

a. Variable cost variances are determined by calculating actual costs and comparing them to standard or budgeted costs previously developed. Standard costs are normally determined by multiplying the standard quantity (i.e., units or some other physical measure) of an input by its predetermined standard or budget cost. Two general types of variances that are most often used are:

Price variance, calculated as follows:

Actual quantity × [standard cost – actual cost]

Quantity variance, calculated as follows:

Standard cost × [standard quantity – actual quantity]

Price variances and quantity variances can be calculated for all variable manufacturing related cost items—direct labor, direct materials, and the variable portion of manufacturing overhead. However, these variances may be called by different names as indicated in the following table:

Price and quantity variances

Price variance equivalents	Quantity variance equivalents
Material price variance	Material usage variance
Labor rate variance	Labor efficiency variance
Variable overhead spending variance	Variable overhead efficiency variance

Example of variance calculations:

Material variances:

Budget: 1,000 pieces at $10.00/piece = $10,000
Actual: 950 pieces at $9.80/piece = $9,310
Total material variance = $690 Favorable

Analysis:

Material price variance
= actual quantity [standard cost – actual cost]
= 950 [10.00 – 9.80] = 950 × 0.20 = $190 Favorable
Material usage variance
= standard cost [standard quantity – actual quantity]
= $10.00 [1,000 – 950] = $10.00 × 50 = $500 Favorable.
Total material variance = $690 Favorable

Labor variances:

Budget: 2,400 hours at $8.50/hour = $20,400

Actual: 2,450 hours at $8.60/hour = $21,070

Total labor variance = $670 Unfavorable

Analysis:

Labor rate variance

= actual hours [standard rate – actual rate]

= 2,450 [8.50 – 8.60] = 2,450 × 0.10 = $245 Unfavorable

Labor efficiency variance

= standard rate [standard hours – actual hours]

– $8.50 [2,400 – 2,450] = $8.50 × –50 = $425 Unfavorable.

Total labor variance = $670 Unfavorable.

Variable overhead variances:

Budget: 2,400 labor hours at $10.50/hour = $ 25,200

Actual: 2,450 labor hours at $10.60/hour = $25,970

Total variable overhead variance = $770 Unfavorable

Analysis:

Variable overhead spending variance

= actual hours [standard rate – actual rate]

= 2,450 [10.50 – 10.60] = 2,450 × 0.10 = $245 Unfavorable

Variable overhead efficiency variance

= standard rate [standard hours – actual hours]

= $10.50 [2,400 – 2,450] = $10.50 × 50 = $525 Unfavorable.

Total variable overhead variance = $770 Unfavorable

b. Fixed cost variances: These can also be calculated simply by comparing the actual costs incurred to the budgeted costs. Because the focus is on fixed costs, however, flexible budgeting procedures are not relevant. Fixed cost variances generated are referred to as spending (or budget) variances or volume variances.

Example of variance calculations:

Fixed overhead variances

Budget—based on 2,400 labor hours = $15,000

Actual = $14,500

Total fixed overhead variance = $500 Favorable

Analysis:

Fixed overhead – volume variance

= standard rate [standard hours – actual hours]

= $6.25 [2,400 – 2,450] = $6.25 × –50 = $312 Unfavorable

Fixed overhead – spending (or budget) variance

= allowed overhead – actual overhead

= [$6.25 × 2,450] – $14,500 = $15,312 – $14,500

= $812 Favorable

Total fixed overhead variance = $500 Favorable

Volume variances arise because fixed overhead costs are independent of the level of business activity, but are applied for costing purposes as though they were variable (e.g. $15,000/2,400 labor hours = $6.25/hour in the immediately preceding example). Because of the fact that fixed costs do not, by definition, vary with changes in activity, management must realize that any volume variance generated is not controllable—it is merely a means of identifying how much of the variance is caused by the cost system itself because of volume changes from budgeted levels.

Fixed cost expense control must be handled differently from variable and semi-variable costs. Actual cost comparison related directly to budgeted figures, independent of activity level, represents the simplest method. You must also keep in mind that many fixed costs are not controllable because they have been committed to or are handled higher up in the organization structure, perhaps at a corporate office far removed from the facility or activity under scrutiny.

Profit Center Performance Evaluation

Segment reporting is the process of reporting activities of various segments of an organization, such as profit centers or product lines. While variance analysis is often used as a basis for evaluating results of profit center performance, the contribution approach to profitability is also frequently employed. The contribution approach is useful in this kind of segmental reporting because it utilizes cost behavior patterns, focuses on the controllable costs, and can be used for evaluating performance as well as decision making. Contribution analysis encompasses the following concepts and definitions:

- Variable costs are more controllable than fixed costs as volume levels change.
- There is a difference between direct costs and indirect costs (shared costs) that must be clearly identified. Direct costs relate specifically to the individual profit center, but indirect costs are shared by the entire organization and cannot be directly related to a specific profit center.
- Contribution margin = sales less all variable costs – manufacturing, selling, and administrative costs.
- Contribution controllable by segment = contribution margin less direct fixed costs (i.e, engineering, research, sales promotions, etc.)
- Segment margin = contribution controllable by segment less fixed costs not controllable by the profit center (i.e, depreciation, property taxes, insurance, etc.)
- Net income = segment margin less unallocated common fixed costs (i.e., home office allocations, corporate research and development (R&D), etc.)

Example:

	Total $	Segment 1 $	Segment 2 $
Sales	300,000	180,000	120,000
Total variable costs	130,000	82,000	48,000
Contribution margin	170,000	98,000	72,000
Less direct fixed controllable costs	47,000	28,000	19,000
Contribution controllable by segment	123,000	70,000	53,000
Less fixed costs not controllable by segment	27,000	16,000	11,000
Segment margin	96,000	54,000	42,000
Less unallocated fixed costs	34,000	n/a	n/a
Net income	62,000		

Use of this method of reporting, or a variation suited to the specific needs of the business, allows measurement of performance to be made at different levels within the range of operating activities. A segment manager can be held accountable for all results down to the contribution controllable by segment, and his or her compensation can be readily tied in whole or in part to this subtotal as well. The economic viability of the entire segment can be examined by looking at the segment margin. And the overall impact of unallocated common fixed costs can be isolated and examined separately from the results of the operating segments.

While the particular format presented here may not be suitable for every business, the concept of segregating by controllability and identifying results by logical entities within the overall organization is appropriate for most businesses. Critical examination of the business will point out which elements are controllable by whom, and statements can be prepared to identify results at different levels of accountability. This kind of analytical process represents the essence of responsibility accounting.

Investment Center Performance Evaluation

The two most widely used measures of performance for the investment center are ROI and RI.

a. ROI is a generic term and can be calculated in many ways. Two of the most common are return on assets (ROA) and return on equity (ROE). Both relate profitability to invested capital as follows:

$$ROA = \frac{\text{Operating Income}}{\text{Operating Assets}}$$

$$ROE = \frac{\text{Net Income}}{\text{Stockholders' Equity}}$$

To evaluate investment center performance, the ROA approach is more suitable and more commonly used because it relates return from the operations of the business (operating income) to the resources (operating assets) used to generate that return, that is, it measures operating efficiency. ROE is more appropriate as a calculation of investment return to stockholders than as an operating standard, that is, it measures investment effectiveness.

Two concepts that are used to enhance and expand the ROI calculations are:

1. margin, which is a measure of profitability or operating efficiency; and
2. turnover, which measures how well resources have been managed and utilized.

Example:

Investment center A produced the following financial results:

Sales	$340,000
Operating income	31,000
Operating assets	240,000

$$\text{ROA} = \frac{\text{Operating Income}}{\text{Operating Assets}} = \frac{31,000}{240,000} = 12.92\%$$

Alternatively, the calculation could be made as follows:

$$\text{Margin} = \frac{\text{Operating Income}}{\text{Sales}} = \frac{31,000}{340,000} = 9.12\%$$

$$\text{Turnover} = \frac{\text{Sales}}{\text{Operating Assets}} = \frac{340,000}{240,000} = 1.417 \text{ times}$$

$$\text{ROI} = \text{margin} \times \text{turnover} = 9.12\% \times 1.417 \text{ times} = 12.92\%$$

The separation of ROI into margin and turnover segments provides several advantages over the straight ROI formula relative to profit planning. Among the advantages:

- Turnover is emphasized as an important element of overall ROI.
- Sales, which are not explicitly included in the basic ROI formula, are recognized as a key factor to evaluate.
- Separating margin and turnover highlights the possibility of trading off one for the other to improve investment center operations (note that a weak margin can be complemented by a strong turnover and vice versa to arrive at the same ROI).

The division of ROI into margin and turnover can also assist management in planning for profit improvement (profit planning process) by showing the impact of

- improved margin, that is, reducing expenses, raising selling prices, and increasing sales faster than expenses;
- improved turnover, that is, increasing sales and holding assets relatively constant, or reducing assets while holding sales constant;
- improved margin and turnover, that is, various combinations of increased selling prices, reduced expenses, and reduced assets.

b. RI is the operating income that the investment center earns above some minimum acceptable rate of return on its operating assets. Note that RI, unlike ROI, is an absolute amount of income and not a percentage rate of return. When RI is used to evaluate an investment center's performance, the evaluative measure is the total amount of RI (i.e., profit rather than profitability). The calculation is made as follows:

$$RI = \text{Operating income} - [\text{minimum required rate of return} \times \text{operating assets}]$$

To illustrate, for investment center A discussed previously, assuming a minimum required rate of return of 12 percent:

$$RI = \$31,000 - (12\% \times \$240,000) = 31,000 - 28,800 = \$2,200$$

RI is regarded by some as a better measure of performance than ROI, because it can lead to investments in projects that an ROI approach might reject. Under ROI, managers generally must accept only investments with returns equal to or greater than the organization's targeted ROI (referred to as the *hurdle rate*). Otherwise the investment will decrease the overall ROI of the business. Often, the hurdle rate is set at unrealistically high levels for reasons of conserving capital, upper management's financial conservatism, or a misguided sense of how high a return the organization should be getting. Using RI, managers would accept an investment if it were expected to earn a rate in excess of the minimum required rate of return (possibly the hurdle rate), thus adding to the overall organizational RI.

On the other hand, the RI approach favors larger investments over smaller projects that might have higher percentage rates of return, because bigger investments generate relatively higher amounts of RI by virtue of the larger amount of capital involved. The choice, then, between the two methods is a matter for management to determine depending on their concept of what is most important to the organization and its various constituents.

Reporting

The reporting process in an organization tends to have little attention paid to it unless it is unsatisfactory to the recipients, in which case, the process attracts considerable unsolicited criticism. Good reporting can do wondrous things in communicating a message to the recipient, while poor reporting can be doubly negative in its impact: First because the report may have unusable or incorrect information and thereby lead to improper decisions; and second, because poor reports, even if accurate, can cause the reader to turn away in frustration if the information wanted is not clearly presented.

1. Report concepts and features

    There are a number of reporting concepts that should become an integral part of the thinking of those who prepare reports for the rest of the organization. These include

    a. *Exception reporting*: Highlighting only those areas requiring management attention. Managers tend to be overwhelmed with data that require no action. A reporting system that directs attention specifically to those items requiring managerial intervention or action can be a significant time saver and can substantively improve managerial effectiveness;

    b. *Flexible budget reporting*: Directed toward a range rather than a single level of activity, it uses budgets that can be adjusted to reflect changes due to variations in activity;

    c. *Summarized reporting*: Providing information for each level within the organization that the managers at that level need to know to effectively manage their operations, but avoiding irrelevant and unnecessary information outside their control or responsibility;

d. *Comparative reporting:* Information in isolation has limited mean-ing, so there must be standards against which to compare operat-ing results. For example:

- Budget versus actual
- This year versus prior year(s)
- Standard costs and revenues
- Company goals and objectives
- External comparisons such as industry standards or com-petitors' results

e. *Interpretive reporting:* Providing substantive analytical commen-tary whenever possible in order to help the recipient understand the significance of the information.

EFFECTIVE REPORTING
PRODUCES EFFECTIVE COMMUNICATION

---

f. *Real-time reporting:* With a PC or data terminal sitting on almost every employee's desk or work station, there exists the technical ability to provide exception or suspect messages instantaneously on the computer monitor (with an audible or flashing signal) while the transaction is happening. Such real-time reporting ena-bles the designated user to take immediate action to determine what specifically has happened, what needs to be done, the effect on operations, what corrective action to take, and the cause of the situation so that it doesn't continue to happen;

g. *Pyramid reporting process:* Management reporting, such as respon-sibility accounting and reporting by exception, to be effective, should be on a pyramid or hierarchical reporting basis. Under this concept top management receives overview or summary reports, and each succeeding level of management gets reports with increasing levels of detail and narrowing scope.

REAL-TIME REPORTING
FIX THE CAUSE, NOT THE BLAME

Certain features that should be part of any reporting process include the following:

- *Timeliness*: In the same way that yesterday's newspaper is deemed valueless, reports that appear too long after the fact are looked upon with justifiable scorn and frustration.
- *Accuracy*: While self-evident, accuracy cannot always be taken for granted. Inaccurate reports not only can give misleading information but can also damage the credibility of future reports.
- *Usefulness*: Again, self-evident, but not always followed. The information in reports must serve the needs of the recipient or it will be ignored.
- *Comfortable terminology*: Reports are designed to benefit the user, and the presenter preparing the presentation should keep that in mind. Avoid jargon and complex terminology as much as possible so that the user will be able to concentrate on the substance of the message rather than having to spend unnecessary time unraveling its meaning.
- *Cost effectiveness*: A report that takes hours of human, computer time, or both to prepare and then presents information of minimal value to the recipient is not effective utilization of corporate resources. Consider the benefit of the report relative to the cost to prepare it before launching a major effort to get it out just because someone asked for it. People often make requests without being aware of the cost of the effort to comply, and it is appropriate to make that effort known to the requester before complying.
- *Clear presentation*: Garbled information or illogical presentation will make it almost impossible for the recipient to understand the information in the report, in which case the report will go unheeded and its preparation will represent wasted effort.
- *Precision versus accuracy*: These terms are not synonymous. A report can be prepared to the nearest thousand units or dollars and be sufficiently accurate for the user. The cost outlay for

more precise (detailed) information should only be undertaken if the results warrant the expenditure.

- *Standardization*: Consistent formats and methods of presentation will help recipients to understand the information presented and will make it easier for them to take appropriate action.

Financial Statement Analysis

One needs to look at the process of appraising the business's situation—from both a financial as well as an operational basis—as to determine the level of operational reporting in place, which needs to be implemented, and which areas of the business need to be improved. Typically, the external Certified Public Accountant (CPA) exercises due diligence by ensuring that the value of the internal and reporting controls are in place based on asset valuation and income potential as a going-concern business, and the accuracy and reliability of the numbers presented on the business's financial statements, such as

- balance sheet;
- income statement.

In those instances, where the business is privately held, many times family owned and operated, the business is subject to greater owner manipulation with less reliance on proper internal controls and reporting than a larger publicly held company that is subject to stricter SEC legislation and Sarbanes–Oxley requirements. Such a privately held company may operate in a manner that produces questionable nontaxable business expenses that go into the owners' pockets. In addition, there may be unreported cash sales and unreported inventory withdrawals that are in reality proper business transactions that should be recorded in the financial records as such. These factors have an impact on the company's current and continuing operations and must be considered in the development of reporting controls.

The business may have his or her own financial personnel to prepare internal statements, but more likely will hire outside financial experts such as a CPA firm to prepare its final formal financial statements. The CPA may reconcile accounts, confirm balances with vendors and customers, and verify that transactions such as sales and accounts receivable are legitimate and other tests of the financial records that they deem appropriate. While they may review the company's operations and note some deficiencies, their emphasis is normally focused on financial not operating procedures. Such an emphasis must be moved from the focus on accounting records only to the business operations behind the financial numbers.

MOVE THE FOCUS FROM ACCOUNTING RECORDS TO THE OPERATIONS BEHIND THE NUMBERS

The Business's Financial Numbers

Let's look at a sample set of financial statements as shown in the balance sheet and income statements shown in the following table. Typically, these amounts will be reviewed as to their validity and whether the business can rely on them as a basis for valuing the business's financial position. In addition, these amounts and operating trends as shown on the following statements should be analyzed as to producing reliable financial records from proper and efficient operations and internal controls.

Comparative balance sheets as of December 31
(Figures in thousands of dollars)

	xxx1	xxx2	xxx3
Assets			
Cash	100	450	400
Marketable securities	0	500	300
Accounts receivable	1,900	1,600	1,700
Inventory	2,200	1,650	1,600
Current assets	4,200	4,200	4,000
Property, plant, equipment	6,500	3,100	2,800
Total assets	10,700	7,300	6,800
Liabilities and equity			
Accounts payable	1,350	900	750
Other payables	400	350	500
Current liabilities	1,750	1,250	1,250
Long-term debt	3,250	1,100	1,250

(Continued)

	xxx1	xxx2	xxx3
Total liabilities	5,000	2,350	2,500
Paid-in-capital	2,200	2,200	2,200
Retained earnings	3,500	2,750	2,100
Total equity	5,700	4,950	4,300
Total liabilities and equity	10,700	7,300	6,800

Comparative income statements for the years ended December 31
(Figures in thousands of dollars)

	xxx1	xxx2	xxx3
Net sales	12,500	11,000	10,500
Cost of goods sold			
Materials	3,500	2,400	1,600
Labor	2,200	2,700	3,200
Manufacturing expenses	2,400	2,200	2,000
Total Cost of goods sold	8,100	7,300	6,800
Manufacturing profit	4,400	3,700	3,700
Selling expenses	1,200	1,050	1,100
General and administrative expenses	1,200	1,300	1,200
Total operating expenses	2,400	2,350	2,300
Net income	2,000	1,350	1,400

Analysis of Financial Statements

The analysis of the company's balance sheet and income statement, besides validating the numbers, might disclose the following concerns.

Balance Sheet

Assets

> *Cash management:* Shows a decrease in cash (from $400 to $450 to $100) with a corresponding sell-off of marketable securities. This is an indication of sacrificing short-term liquidity, making the company vulnerable to cash demands, while investing in long-term property, plant, and equipment—hoping for a favorable ROI. The company barely has enough cash to operate safely on a daily basis and has greatly sacrificed its buffer cash position for emergencies,

necessities, and opportunities. They have also maximized their use of accounts payable to satisfy their immediate and short-term operating needs. They have placed themselves in a vulnerable position, ripe for a reasonable offer.

Accounts receivable: Shows an increase of 18 percent from $1,600 to $1,900. Based on industry and company norms, this could also be large in relation to sales ($12,500/$1,900 = 6.58 percent). The increase in sales, but not necessarily in collections, has resulted in some corresponding increase in accounts receivable. However, these sales need to be analyzed to determine the presence of poor operating practices such as

- selling excessively to present customers far beyond reasonable credit limits;
- selling to new customers of a questionable nature;
- selling inventory at mark-down prices to make the sale and turn inventory into cash.

This situation could also indicate ineffective billing and collection procedures.

Inventory: Shows an increase of 33 percent from $1,650 to $2,200. Possibly, to justify the business's long-term capital investment, and once all possible sales have been exhausted, there is still excess capacity, and so the business produces to inventory. This could also indicate weaknesses in inventory control and related purchasing, vendor relations, and receiving and storeroom procedures.

Property, plant, and equipment: Shows a large increase of 110 percent from $3,100 to $6,500 indicating large recent expansion that may have been unnecessary, controlled ineffectively, or used improperly. Based on the decision to invest long term, it appears that the business is trying to operationally justify its decision by hyping sales and creating inventory, while devastating its balance sheet.

Liabilities:

Accounts payable: Shows an increase of 50 percent from $900 to $1,350 indicating unnecessary purchasing, overextension of expenditures, and weakened ability to pay. Reliance on vendors, especially those critical to its operations has been weakened, with resultant increases in prices, cash only policies, and cut-offs of materials. Going to other vendors has resulted in price increases with a resultant stoppage in supply lines.

Long-term debt: Shows a large increase of almost 300 percent from $1,100 to $3,250 that indicates substantial changes in the business resulting in increased property, plant, and equipment with corresponding decrease in the business's cash position. It is questionable as to whether the business can justify its decision with any semblance of an adequate ROI. To take this on is a severe burden to the company. The owners and management have to be certain that the business can handle such long-term debt, correct the cash management situation, and produce an adequate ROI.

Retained earnings: Shows an increase of $650 and $750 for the two years that indicate that the business has increased their net income as the result of the changes previously noted. It needs to be determined whether this is real net income that can be collected or merely booking of sales and accounts receivables. Also, is this a significant expected change and should the business have been able to do even better?

Income Statement

Sales: Sales have increased from $10,500 to $11,000 to $12,500 over the past three years. Analysis by product line should be made to determine the causes for such an increase in sales. Should they have done better, are they all good sales, are they selling to less than desirable customers, and exceeding realistic customer credit limits? Looking at the entire situation, this is inadequate real growth to justify the devastation of the balance sheet.

Cost of goods sold: Has increased in total from $6,800 to $7,300 to $8,100. However, material costs are the major contributor to this increase indicating a possible major critical operational area. Factors responsible include price increases, increased production, increased scrap, rejects and rework, inability to pay timely, and material wastage due to learning curve of new equipment (and possible employee sabotage). In addition, labor costs have decreased over the last three years (from $3,200 to $2,200). This indicates a possible shift in manufacturing, but has the business reduced labor and increased productivity to the extent possible using the new equipment.

> **DOING THE RIGHT THING,**
> **THE RIGHT WAY,**
> **AT THE RIGHT COST**

Using Financial Data in Operations

Effective decision making for the business is dependent on reliable and useful information, which may not be forthcoming if all operating transactions are not recorded in the business's books and records. The internal accountant or bookkeeper, and the external CPA, are not the decision makers for the business—especially related to operational concerns and controls. While the internal accountant and the external CPA may provide basic financial information to the business, it must also be determined what else to include in the financial (and operational) information provided to the owners and managers—those who make the operating fixes. Through the providing of the correct operational reporting, this information becomes a crucial contributor to business management in the operational problem solving process. Careful analysis, intelligent problem identification, and accurate assessment of the financial and operational information and controls can guide the business in the right direction.

> **FINANCIAL DATA MUST BE CONVERTED**
> **TO OPERATIONAL DATA TO BE MOST USEFUL**

Analysis of Financial Information

Financial information is usually the starting point for analyzing the business's operations as to how they operate and what controls should be established to ensure effective management over all of their activities. Financial statement and reporting analysis is an effective tool to analyze the business's operations and reported results. If done properly, useful information about the business's financial status and trends, as well as operational considerations, can result in assisting the business in establishing effective plans for future growth.

If management understands the basic purposes and principles for the business being in existence, management (sometimes with outside assistance) can help the business identify why it has gone astray and what can be done to get it back on the right track. In addition, the owners and management must understand the significance of reported financial and operational information, how to interpret such information, and what steps need to be taken to address those areas of positive improvement as well as those operational areas in need of improvement and change.

IT'S NOT THE REPORTING OF INFORMATION BUT THE REVIEW AND ANALYSIS OF INFORMATION

A good starting point for such business operational analysis is the timely preparation, analysis, and review of financial statements produced from controlled business transactions that ensure that all transactions are recorded accurately and that no transactions are lost or omitted. However, additional financial and operational data is needed for the business to obtain an all-encompassing picture of what is happening in the business. Remember that every financial transaction processed and reported is the result of some operational activity—accordingly both financial and operational activities need to be reviewed and analyzed.

The analysis of financial information is the key to what operational areas should be controlled and reported to management. Improving a deficient operational area leads to improving the related financial transactions and reporting.

FINANCIAL INFORMATION EMANATES FROM OPERATIONS

Exercise:

Consider the following income statement for the Example company. What problems do you see and what additional information would you want to be able to analyze the situation further?

The Example company—Results of operations
Level 1 report—Summary

Date: DECEMBER

Example company—income statement
($ in thousands)

Account description	Current month Budget $	Current month Actual $	Current month Variance better (worse) than budget $	Current month Variance better (worse) than budget %	Year to date Actual $	Year to date Budget $	Year to date Variance better (worse) than budget $	Year to date Variance better (worse) than budget %
Sales	4,660	4,615	(45)	(1.0)	55,514	55,900	(386)	(0.7)
Cost of goods sold	2,610	3,726	(1,116)	(42.8)	33,057	31,300	(1,757)	(5.6)
Gross profit	2,050	889	(1,161)	(56.6)	22,457	24,600	(2,143)	(8.7)
Selling, general and admin.	937	935	2	0.2	11,380	11,250	(130)	(1.2)
Operating profit	1,113	(46)	(1,159)	(104.1)	11,077	13,350	(2,273)	(17.0)
Other income (expense)	(25)	(24)	1	4.0	(288)	(290)	2	0.7
Profit before taxes	1,088	(70)	(1,158)	(106.4)	10,789	13,060	(2,271)	(17.4)
Provision for income taxes	365	(24)	389	(106.6)	3,600	4,360	760	17.4
Net Income (loss)	723	(46)	(769)	(106.4)	7,189	8,700	(1,511)	(17.4)

Now let's use the principles of pyramid reporting and attempt to determine the cause of the unfavorable variance in operating profit by reviewing the following detail reports:

Level 2 report—**Detail**

Date: DECEMBER

Operating income summary by division
($ in thousands)

Current month				Account description	Year to date			
Variance better (worse) than budget		Budget	Actual		Actual	Budget	Variance better (worse) than budget	
%	$	$	$		$	$	$	%
0.8	1	121	122	Operating income—div. A	1,468	1,450	18	1.2
(122.7)	(1,156)	942	(214)	Operating income—div. B	9,059	11,300	(2,241)	(19.8)
(8.0)	(4)	50	46	Operating income—div. C	550	600	(50)	(8.3)
(104.1)	(1,159)	1,113	(46)	Total operating income	11,077	13,350	(2,273)	(17.0)

Level 3 report—**Detail**

Date: DECEMBER

Operating income statement—division B
($ in thousands)

| | Current month | | | Account description | | Year to date | | |
| Variance better (worse) than budget | | Budget | Actual | | Actual | Budget | Variance better (worse) than budget | |
%	$	$	$		$	$	$	%
(1.6)	(60)	3,750	3,690	Sales	44,812	45,000	(188)	(0.4)
(52.7)	(1,099)	2,085	3,184	Cost of goods sold	26,928	25,000	(1,928)	(7.7)
(69.6)	(1,159)	1,665	506	Gross profit	17,884	20,000	(2,116)	(10.6)
(1.5)	(5)	335	340	Selling expenses	4,108	4,000	(108)	(2.7)
2.1	8	388	380	Administrative expenses	4,717	4,700	(17)	(0.4)
(122.7)	(1,156)	942	(214)	Operating profit	9,059	11,300	(2,241)	(19.8)

Level 4 report—**Detail**

Date: DECEMBER

Cost of goods sold—Division B
($ in thousands)

	Current month			Account description	Year to date		
Variance better (worse) than budget		Budget	Actual		Actual	Budget	Variance better (worse) than budget
%	$	$	$		$	$	$	%
3.3	25	765	740	Material usage	8,980	9,200	220	2.4
(2.7)	(12)	440	452	Direct labor	5,354	5,300	(54)	(1.0)
(3.8)	(8)	210	218	Direct overhead	2,692	2,500	(192)	(7.7)
(164.8)	(1,104)	670	1,774	Indirect overhead	9,902	8,000	(1,902)	(23.8)
(52.7)	(1,099)	2,085	3,184	Total cost of goods sold	26,928	25,000	(1,928)	(7.7)

Level 5 report—**Detail**

Date: DECEMBER

Indirect overhead—Division B
($ in thousands)

Current month				Account description	Year to date			
Variance better (worse) than budget		Budget	Actual		Actual	Budget	Variance better (worse) than budget	
%	$	$	$		$	$	$	%
(13.3)	(20)	150	170	Supervision salaries	2,070	1,800	(270)	(15.0)
(2.4)	(5)	210	215	Fringe benefits	2,580	2,500	(80)	(3.2)
0	0	95	95	Depreciation	1,140	1,100	(40)	(3.6)
(3.1)	(2)	65	67	Rent	810	800	(10)	(1.3)
(1,256.)	(1,068)	85	1,153	Maintenance and repairs	2,356	1,000	(1,356)	(135.6)
(12.5)	(5)	40	45	Supplies	550	500	(50)	(10.0)
(33.3)	(5)	15	20	Insurance	290	200	(90)	(45.0)
10.0	1	10	9	Miscellaneous	106	100	(6)	(6.0)
(164.8)	(1,104)	670	1,774	Total indirect overhead	9,902	8,000	(1,902)	(23.8)

Level 6 report—**Detail**

Date: DECEMBER

Maintenance department—Division B
($ in thousands)

Current month				Account description	Year to date			
Variance better (worse) than budget		Budget	Actual		Actual	Budget	Variance better (worse) than budget	
%	$	$	$		$	$	$	%
(6.7)	(2)	30	32	Wages	425	350	(75)	(21.4)
(20.0)	(1)	5	6	Salaries	70	60	(10)	(16.7)
(16.7)	(2)	12	14	Fringe benefits	170	140	(30)	(21.4)
(4,077.)	(1,060)	26	1,086	Outside contracts	1,492	310	(1,182)	(381.3)
(28.6)	(2)	7	9	Supplies	125	80	(45)	(56.3)
(25.0)	(1)	4	5	Tools	62	50	(12)	(24.0)
0	0	1	1	Miscellaneous	12	10	(2)	(20.0)
(1,256.)	(1,068)	85	1,153	Total maintenance department	2,356	1,000	(1,356)	(135.6)

Level 7 report—**Specific expenditures**
Detail of Outside Contracts Account

Date	Vendor	Amount
01/15/	Certain supply	$15,632.28
01/28/	Tyte controls	$24,500.00
02/07/	Hothands electric	$44,276.89
03/19/	Plugit heating and plumbing	$28,803.00
04/30/	Cool-aire air conditioning, Inc.	$108,477.43
05/15/	Cleen-sweep Janitorial	$38,613.90
05/31/	Allrattle auto	$18,975.58
08/19/	Sure foot roofing	$27,824.12
09/26/	Cover-up painting, Inc.	$98,892.00
12/05/	Fixxup equipment maintenance	$26,270.15
12/23/	Lucky eddie's game shoppe	$1,060,213.07
	Total	$1,492,478.42

Level 8 report—Analysis and interpretation

To: Board of Directors

From: Thomas T. Tikkers, Tikkers and Chekkers, CPAs

Re: December operating results   Date: January 14

During the month of December the company experienced an operating loss of $46,000 compared to a budgeted profit of $1,113,000. Division B's operating loss for the month was $214,000. This represented an unfavorable variance from budget of $1,156,000, which accounts for virtually all of the company's total variance for the month. December's results for Division B caused its year to date variance to double to a total of $2,241,000. Upon careful investigation, it was found that the cause of the deviation could be principally attributed to an unauthorized expenditure by the maintenance department of $1,060,000 for a Christmas party fete which included extravagant food, an incomprehensible amount of liquor, casino gambling activities, and various other forms of *entertainment* which cannot in good taste be detailed in this memo. At our recommendation, the company has taken immediate disciplinary steps to deal with the situation as follows:

1. Ken I. Fixxit, maintenance department supervisor has been dismissed for permitting the company to sponsor illegal and unauthorized activities. The company is considering legal action.

2. R. Leader, division B general manager has been removed from his former position for not being aware of the maintenance department activities and allowing the expenditures to pass through for payment. He is now assistant foreman of the motor pool.

3. Tom Debit, division B controller has been fired for not having adequate controls in place to prevent the unauthorized expenditure from happening.

4. Evan Balance, corporate controller, has been demoted to the position of data entry operator, class I.

5. B.I.G. Bucks, former chief financial officer, has been persuaded to take early retirement. He can be reached care of general delivery, Rio de Janeiro, Brazil, where he has entered into partnership with a local businessman, Eduardo Fortunato.

We believe that these actions show the firm commitment of your company's management to running a tight ship and a willingness to take whatever steps are necessary, no matter how unpleasant, to protect the welfare of its shareholders.

Budget Reporting and Control

They say that budgeting and budget reporting is easy for management. You merely take last year's budget and decide by what percentage to increase or decrease (in today's economy this is the more normal) each department and function's budget. Then each month you have the assigned individual or group, typically someone from the accounting or controller's function, review the budget versus actual reports to ensure that all areas operate within the budget. If there is a deficiency, usually an area approaching or going over the budget within a line item such as personnel, materials, or supplies there is usually some form of reprimand and orders from above as to stopping expenditures. There may be no relationship to the organizational plans or expected results—only that the budget has been exceeded. And many times the manager who is able to have his or her budget increased year after year is considered the hero as more power and control is endowed upon them—resulting in being rewarded for increasing your budget.

An effective planning and budgeting process takes the opposite approach, that is, to make the planning and budget, one of identifying best practices and operating most economically, efficiently, and effectively—and rewarding those who reduce their budgets (or display how they can reduce or even eliminate their functions and activities) in a program of continuous improvement in an organizational learning environment. In such a learning environment, reporting and control becomes real time reporting of variance items so that immediate remedial action can be taken to correct the situation and ensure that it doesn't happen again. To be most effective, employees need to be delegated the authority and responsibility over those results that they are held accountable to produce. For optimum results each employee needs to be given the permission to be themselves and the permission to fail and learn by their mistakes—in effect putting each employee in business for him or herself. Compensation and rewards then become based on the objective achievement of results, and the planning, budgeting, and reporting and control system becomes once again a helpful system rather than a punitive one.

The control and monitoring process focuses on the progress and completion of agreed upon steps within the detail plans with the budget becoming the dollar manifestation of the cost of the detail plan steps. As the detail plan changes in scope, as to an increase or decrease in activity or cost, so must the budget change under the concept of flexible budgeting. As the detail plan succeeds, hopefully using less monetary resources than anticipated, the excess budgeted funds are transferred—to another detail plan or where else funds are needed. With detail plan success, the organization moves closer to accomplishing departmental goals and objectives, organizational goals and objectives, long-term goals, and strategic thrusts that increase the company's competitive advantage.

**REPORTING AND CONTROLLING
HELP TO MAKE PLANNING AND BUDGETING
A HELPFUL SYSTEM**

About the Author

Rob Reider, CPA, MBA, PhD, is the president of Reider Associates, a management and organizational consulting firm located in Santa Fe, New Mexico, that he founded in January 1976. Rob is a nationally recognized author, speaker, seminar leader and management consultant. He has provided consulting services to numerous private and public industries in a multiple of disciplines. Rob has published numerous articles in professional journals and has been a presenter at various professional meetings and conferences. He is the author of nine professional management books and five works of fiction. Rob resides in Santa Fe, NM with his wife Barbara. He can be contacted via email at: robreider1@gmail.com

Other Books by Rob Reider

Business and Management Books

Benchmarking Strategies: A Tool for Profit Improvement
Effective Operations & Controls for the Small Privately Held Business
Improving the Economy, Efficiency, and Effectiveness of Not-For-Profits
Managing Cash Flow: An Operational Focus (with Peter B. Heyler)
Operational Review: Maximum Results at Efficient Costs
Operational Review: Workbook (Case studies, forms, and exercises)
Expanding Customer Service as a Profit Center
The Search for Best Practices

Fiction

American Scream: A Novel of Hope and Possibilities
Brother Knot: A Novel of Oppression's Effect on the Other
Creating an Authentic Life: The Storyteller and the Tale of Self
Gone Wanting: A Novel of Unfulfilled Dreams and Living with Reality
Road to Oblivion: The Footpath Back Home (a novel of discovery)

Index

OTHER TITLES IN THE STRATEGIC MANAGEMENT COLLECTION

William Q. Judge, Old Dominion University, Editor

FORTHCOMING IN THIS COLLECTION

Announcing the Business Expert Press Digital Library

Concise e-books business students need for classroom and research

This book can also be purchased in an e-book collection by your library as

- a one-time purchase,
- that is owned forever,
- allows for simultaneous readers,
- has no restrictions on printing, and
- can be downloaded as PDFs from within the library community.

Our digital library collections are a great solution to beat the rising cost of textbooks. E-books can be loaded into their course management systems or onto students' e-book readers.
The **Business Expert Press** digital libraries are very affordable, with no obligation to buy in future years. For more information, please visit **www.businessexpertpress.com/librarians**. To set up a trial in the United States, please email **sales@businessexpertpress.com**.

www.ingramcontent.com/pod-product-compliance
Lightning Source LLC
Chambersburg PA
CBHW060603210326
41519CB00014B/3552